Steiner

**Financial Checks on Soviet
Defense Expenditures**

# Financial Checks on Soviet Defense Expenditures

**Franklyn D. Holzman**
Tufts University

**Lexington Books**
D.C. Heath and Company
Lexington, Massachusetts
Toronto            London

**Library of Congress Cataloging in Publication Data**

Holzman, Franklyn D
 Financial checks on Soviet defense expenditures.

 Bibliography: p. 99.
 1. Russia—Armed Forces—Appropriations and expenditures.
I. Title.
UA770.H64  354'.47'00895  75-656
ISBN 0-699-97808-6

Published simultaneously in Canada

Printed in the United States of America

International Standard Book Number: 0-669-97808-6

Library of Congress Catalog Card Number: 75-656

*And they shall beat their swords*
*into plowshares,*

*And their spears into pruning-hooks;*

*Nation shall not lift up sword*
*against nation,*

*Neither shall they learn war any*
*more.*

Isaiah 2:4

# Contents

# List of Tables

# Preface

This study was undertaken in the hope that it would contribute to the achievement of peace by facilitating a reduction in Soviet and American military expenditures. The USSR had several times proposed before the United Nations that the major powers agree to reduce their military expenditures by 10 or 15 percent. This proposal, it should be noted, has several virtues which distinguish it from other disarmament or arms control proposals. First, under most other proposals, because the military profiles of nations are so different, it is difficult to get agreement on the extent to which the reductions in various military dimensions in one nation are equivalent to those in another. This is a much less serious problem under the Soviet proposal because each nation chooses its own "reduction mix." Second, since each nation does choose its own "reduction mix," it naturally eliminates those programs to which it accords lowest priority. Thus an initial 10 percent reduction in budgeted military expenditures may reduce military potential by no more than a few percent, if at all (in light of the "fat" that seems to characterize defense establishments). This should reduce resistance to participation and facilitate agreement. Third, if carried out faithfully, the Soviet proposal would result in an actual reduction in the amount of world resources devoted to military purposes. This is not necessarily true of more specialized arms control treaties, since limitations on expenditures in some areas may well be compensated for by increased expenditures in others. In fact, Secretary of Defense James Schlesinger has stated that the Vladivostok Agreement would lead to an increase, rather than decrease, in U.S. defense spending.

In 1964, I was asked by the United States Arms Control and Disarmament Agency to study this type of proposal, particularly to try to deal with some of the obvious obstacles to its adoption by the U.S. Government. More specifically, the study was to attempt the following: to clarify the problems involved in financial verification of reductions in military expenditures in light of the paucity of data provided by the USSR; to spell out the kinds of data that might be required for verification; and, if possible, to devise verification techniques that would be sufficiently unintrusive to be acceptable to the USSR as well as other major nations.

Some readers of this book may feel that it has the tone of an intelligence manual and is intended for use against the USSR. From my standpoint, the first part of the above sentence is true, in the sense that I was subjecting available information to rigorous tests. The second part, however, is false. In order to discover in a convincing way whether verification with a reasonable degree of assurance is possible and to devise means to achieve it, it was necessary to make the strongest possible negative assumptions regarding Soviet motivations to deceive the United States under the aegis of a military expenditure reduction agreement. This should not be taken to imply that the USSR would necessarily make clandestine military expenditures under such an agreement; nor should it be taken to imply that the United States would not. As Becker (1969, p. 146) says, "Military secrecy is the contemporary hallmark of national sovereignty, and it is the rare government that is prepared to dispense information freely on its military establishment." Realism simply requires that one entertain the possibility of deception under an arms control agreement; and agreement may depend on the existence of an effective verification system.

The original study was completed in 1965 at a time when interest in the subject was waning with the escalation of military budgets because of Vietnam. With the revival of interest and a renewed Soviet proposal at the 28th session of the U.N. General Assembly in 1973, and the consequent establishment by the Secretary General of an "Expert Group on the Reduction of Military Budgets" in 1974, it seemed worthwhile to take another look at the problems in light of recent developments. Probably the major new development was the institution of an Economic Reform in the USSR begun in 1965. One of the consequences of this Reform was to have been a substantial decentralization of economic authority and of the channels of economic activity. Some decentralization of channels of activity occurred, but very little of authority. The result is that, while some of our numbers have changed (e.g., relatively more investment is financed through retained profits of enterprises and through bank credit and less directly via the State Budget), there has been no basic change in the system. The problem of verification as approached here is mostly methodological and in this respect the pre- and post-1965 Soviet economies are virtually the same.

When this study was originally written, Western analysts were fairly sanguine about the possibility of determining the possible range of and trends in Soviet military expenditures from careful examination of the various "budget residuals," i.e., unspecified "other expenditure" items in the State Budget. These are considered in the text, as they must be here, and in the Appendix. But it is worth reporting that much less confidence is now placed in this type of analysis.

Many other techniques have been devised to try to determine, among other things, the level of Soviet military expenditures using input-output procedures, industrial production statistics, and, I have no doubt (but also no information on), direct observation by space satellites and intelligence agents. These techniques, along with financial checks, might be used by the United States or other parties to a budgetary agreement to verify compliance with an agreement on a reduction in military spending. No attempt is made here to consider the usefulness of such techniques.

In Chapter 6, a "sampling" technique for verification of military expenditures is proposed. To my knowledge, this is a novel proposal. Although I discussed possible procedures with statisticians, I would like to stress that I am not a statistician and I do not feel that I have come anywhere near exhausting the possibilities of the method proposed. I do think that the method *may* be viewed as relatively unintrusive by governments and it is my hope that those more skilled than I in statistical and auditing techniques may be able to devise improvements to make it even more effective and less intrusive.

A final note to specialists on the Soviet economy: All data are in post-1961 ruble prices.

Lexington, Mass.
December 1974

# Acknowledgments

My greatest debt in writing this book is to Barbara Merguerian. In fact, I agreed to undertake the original study only after she had agreed to help me with the research. Her combination of a profound knowledge of the Soviet budgetary system and statistics with the judgment and dependability of a fine scholar added immeasurably to the quality of the work. I was very fortunate, in updating the manuscript, to be able to prevail upon her to put aside her own research on Russian history and lend me a hand again.

Next, I am indebted to Ruth Sivard, formerly with the U.S. Arms Control and Disarmament Agency, who conceived the idea for the study, encouraged me to undertake it, and in every way possible assisted and encouraged my work. I am happy to acknowledge that the original study was financed by the U.S. Arms Control and Disarmament Agency.

For technical advice on the Soviet financial system, I am much indebted to Abraham Becker, Daniel Gallik, and Raymond Powell. I relied heavily on their relevant writings (listed in the Bibliography), and on numerous occasions saved myself hours of work and thought by dialing their telephone numbers and picking their brains directly.

My colleague Daniel Ounjian patiently helped me with statistical problems; for this help I am grateful. I am also indebted to Sydney Alexander, whose clever use of sampling methods to estimate German war production during World War II inspired Chapter 6. My colleague Geoffrey Kemp read a draft of the manuscript and offered helpful advice. Finally, I had the benefit of Mrs. E. P. Goodwin's typing and editing, by far the best I have experienced in more than thirty years of professional life.

As usual, I alone bear responsibility for errors and omissions.

# 1

## Introduction

### A. The Soviet Proposals to Reduce Military Expenditures

Over the past 25 years, the USSR has many times proposed before the United Nations reductions in budgeted military expenditures. The proposals have always included the U.S. and the USSR but have often included other major nations as well. Typically, the reductions envisaged have been in the range of 10 to 15 percent. It has also been suggested that a part of the savings realized be used to assist the developing nations.

The original proposal was made in 1948. From 1954 through 1964, at least one proposal was made each year. Then followed seven years of silence. On March 30, 1971 Chairman Brezhnev revived the matter in a speech to the Twenty-Fourth Party Congress when he said: "The Soviet Union is prepared to negotiate on the reduction of military expenditures, first of all, by the major nations." Finally, on September 25, 1973, the USSR proposed that the permanent members of the U.N. Security Council "should reduce their military budgets by 10 percent from the 1973 level during the next financial year" (SIPRI, 1974, p. 394). This proposal was accepted by the General Assembly of the U.N., which requested the Secretary-General to prepare a report on it. At this writing (1974), a group of appointed experts is working on the report.

It is noteworthy that, with some minor exceptions, the Soviet proposals have made no provision for verification. In fact, in the 1973 proposal, the USSR explicitly excludes verification of compliance (SIPRI, 1974, p. 394). This proposal also stipulates that budget reductions are to be based on officially published figures. Since the USSR publishes only one figure for defense expenditures, which is generally believed to exclude a number of important categories of military expenditures (as do the budgeted defense figures of all nations), this stipulation was cause for some concern.

The purpose of this study is to clarify the issues involved in an arms control agreement of this type and under the conditions out-lined above. More specifically, an attempt is made to ascertain the problems involved in verification of reductions in military expenditures in light of the paucity of data provided by the USSR, to spell out the kinds of data which might be required for verification, and if possible to devise verification techniques that are sufficiently "unintrusive" to be acceptable to the USSR and other major powers.

## B. Is Financial Verification Possible in Centrally Planned Economies?

A major purpose of this study is to assess the problems involved in verifying reported reductions in Soviet military expenditures. Since financial (monetary) factors or variables play a much smaller role in determining the allocation of resources in centrally planned economies than they do in capitalist economies, it is appropriate to raise the question whether "financial verification" is, in principle, possible. The answer to this question is "yes," for despite the fact that a major part of the resources of the Soviet economy are directly allocated by the planners, the Soviet economy is nevertheless largely a money economy in which almost all commodity flows, including those connected with defense, are reflected in financial flows.[a] This means that if the accounts are made available, financial checks of claimed reductions in military expenditures should, in principle, be possible and adequate.

In fact, because virtually all economic activity is nationalized in the USSR and as a result of comprehensive "central planning," data on military expenditures should be more complete, more systematized, and more available to the authorities than in the West. This should make financial checks, in theory, simpler and more accurate than would ordinarily be possible in a capitalist country.

On the other hand, the more complete control exercised by the state suggests that manipulation of data designed to mislead should

---

[a]That financial flows accompany real flows does not mean that those possessing "means of finance" can bypass planners' allocation orders or outbid them. In the wartime U.S., it was not enough to have had money, one must also have had a ration card if one wished to purchase sugar, for example. Similarly, in the Soviet Union, rationing by planners is the major constraint determining commodity flows, financial adequacy a minor constraint, especially for commodities other than consumers' goods.

be easier in the Soviet Union than, for example, in the United States. We know that budgetary data can be hidden. We have done it. The Manhattan Project and the CIA are cases in point. Very few people knew that the Manhattan Project existed during World War II despite the large sums poured into it through the budget by our Government. Very few people today have any idea how much is spent annually by the CIA or how such funds are hidden in the federal budget. Clandestine operations of this sort are much harder to manage in this country than in the USSR, for several reasons: the restrictions on budgetary appropriation procedures provided by Article I, Section 9 of the Constitution and subsequent statutory amendment;[b] the long and detailed annual Congressional perusals of the proposed budgets, all of which are published; the constant prying by newspapers, scholars, writers, and others, all of whom are free to publish anything they can dig up, even if classified. None of these hazards or restrictions apply to or need be faced by the Soviet leaders.

## C. Soviet Financial Institutions

The Soviet financial system is much simpler than ours. There are only two significant financial institutions, the State Budget and the Gosbank or State Bank. There are also three less important institutions: a network of savings banks, which serve simply as a conduit for siphoning the savings of the population into the budget; a long-term investment (construction) bank, the Stroibank, which extends a small percentage of the loans for capital investment; and the Foreign Trade Bank, which handles foreign trade and foreign currency transactions and now has a number of branches in foreign countries. Unlike major capitalist nations, the USSR does not have the whole range of different kinds of banks, mutual companies, insurance companies, and financial intermediaries, on the one hand, nor does it have, on the other, the equally wide range of financial instruments, stock markets, bond markets, and the like.

The Gosbank is a major financial institution. Not only does it contain the accounts of all enterprises and institutions—which per-

---

[b] It could be argued, in fact, that the hiding of CIA appropriations under other expenditure categories is illegal.

mits it to serve an important control function—it also is responsible for extending most of the short-term credit and some of the long-term credits required by enterprises and organizations. The short-term credits are to finance goods in transit, seasonal production processes and expenses, and other temporary (and sometimes permanent) working capital needs connected with the production and turnover of goods. As the Soviet economy has grown, so have working capital requirements and the amount of short-term credit outstanding. So also have the currency requirements of the country increased, both cash currency used by the population and bank deposit money used in interenterprise transactions.[c] Unlike the Stroibank, which can only extend credits from resources it actually holds or receives from the Budget, the Gosbank can create new currency when the demand for currency for legitimate working capital needs exceeds the supply. For many years, only scattered data from the Balance Sheet of the Gosbank have been available. These are presented for the years 1961 and 1967 in Table 1-1.

The State Budget (Table 1-2) is the second major Soviet financial institution. The State Budget is not the equivalent of our federal budget but rather the sum of our federal, state, and local budgets. The State Budget, along with the Annual Plan, is ratified by the Supreme Soviet every year. This Budget, which is composed of the Union, Republican, and local Soviet budgets, is the focus of fiscal policy because of the centralized nature of planning. For this reason, the State Budget is relatively much larger than our own. It is also larger because so much more of the national investment, health, educational, and research expenditures flow through it than is true of the United States, where the private sector plays a more important role.

The bulk of the budget revenues come from the turnover tax, which is basically a set of excise taxes on consumers' goods, and from payments from profits by state enterprises. Since the enterprises are owned by the state, enterprise profits and payments into the budget are, from an economic standpoint, more like price-increasing sales taxes than taxes on profits or corporate income in a capitalist country. Other revenues consist of a hodge-podge including fees, licenses, inheritance tax, revenues received by state enter-

---

[c] Enterprises don't write checks or pay one another cash. They simply notify the Gosbank of purchases or sales and the Bank in turn credits and debits the appropriate accounts.

**Table 1-1**
**Balance Sheets of the State Bank (billions of rubles)**

|  | Jan. 1, 1961 | Jan. 1, 1967 |
|---|---|---|
| *Assets* | | |
| Short-term loans to enterprises | 41.19 | 72.16 |
| Long-term loans to enterprises and individuals | 2.95 | 6.33 |
| Government bonds, precious metals, foreign exchange, cash, etc. | 5.86 | — |
| Total | 50.00 | — |
| *Liabilities* | | |
| Bank notes, treasury notes | — | — |
| Deposits of: | | |
| Enterprises | 4.68 | 8.24 |
| Collective farms | .88 | 5.22 |
| Other organizations | 1.02 | 1.66 |
| Individuals | — | .13 |
| State Budget | 18.00[a] | — |
| Budget grants for long-term loans | 2.40[a] | 5.10[a] |
| Deposits of other banks | — | — |
| Capital | — | 3.00[a] |
| Total | 50.00 | — |

[a]Estimate.

Source: R. P. Powell "Monetary Statistics," in V. G. Treml and J. P. Hardt, eds., *Soviet Economic Statistics,* © 1967 Duke University Press (Durham, N.C.), p. 404.

prises or organizations which are not on an independent financial basis (like our former postal system), sales of state property, customs, etc.

The major budget expenditure categories are those on the national economy and those for social-cultural measures and science. Financing the National Economy is often presented in breakdowns by sector (industry, agricultural, etc.) and by end-use (investment, subsidies, etc.). Breakdown data are presented in Tables A-1, A-2, and A-3 in the Appendix. Neither Financing the National Economy nor social-cultural expenditures are exhaustive for these respective categories. As we see below, other sources of finance exist. The one figure for defense, it is worth noting, is the only figure ever presented by the USSR.

Finally, unlike most capitalist nations, the USSR State Budget always runs a surplus, for reasons discussed below.

**Table 1-2**
**State Budget of the USSR, 1971 (billions of rubles)**

| | | |
|---|---:|---:|
| *Revenues* | | 166.0 |
| Turnover tax | 54.5 | |
| Enterprise payments from profits | 55.6 | |
| Income taxes on cooperatives and collective farms | 1.4 | |
| Sales of bonds to population | 0.3 | |
| Income taxes on population | 13.7 | |
| Payroll tax for social insurance | 8.8 | |
| Other revenues | 31.7 | |
| *Expenditures* | | 164.2 |
| Financing the national economy | 80.4 | |
| Social-cultural measures and science, including: | 59.4 | |
|     Education and science | 26.3 | |
|     Health | 9.6 | |
|     Social security | 13.6 | |
|     Social insurance | 7.8 | |
| Defense | 17.9 | |
| Administration | 1.8 | |
| Other expenditures | 4.7 | |
| *Budget Surplus* | | 1.8 |

Source: USSR, Tsentral'noe Statisticheskoe Upravlenie, *Narodnoe Khoziaistvo SSSR, 1922-1972*, Moscow: 1972, p. 481.

## D. Method of Procedure

Initially, our purpose will be to identify Soviet defense expenditures. Since it appears that a part of Soviet defense expenditures is at present not identified, and that in the event of an arms control agreement there might be an incentive to withhold additional information, it is necessary to scrutinize the whole Soviet financial system carefully for possible clandestine military expenditures. There are two sides to every financial transaction, a receipt and an expenditure. Because of the gaps in our information on the Soviet financial system, it is necessary for us to look at both sides for clues. We look at the expenditure side for the possibility of clandestine expenditures. Thus budget expenditures, short-term loans by the Gosbank, etc., must all come under scrutiny. This does not complete the job, however. Suppose we have data on funds to be spent but no obvious expenditures. Then it is necessary to follow these funds through until we are able to ascertain their disposition. Thus it is necessary to check on the disposition of the budget surplus, the amortization deduction, retained profits of enterprises, and so forth. Whether we happen to examine a receipts category or an expenditure category first depends entirely on which happens to be more readily available. Naturally, if the expenditure category is available, it is unnecessary to examine the corresponding receipts category *unless* there is some reason to believe that some of the expenditures have not been disclosed. In this case, it is useful to examine receipts as a means of verification.

Those not familiar with the Soviet economy may wonder at certain obvious omissions from the overall financial picture as presented here. No mention is made, for example, of savings banks, or of sales of lottery bonds to the public, or of the balance of consumer income and expenditure. These and other financial items are not mentioned below either because the funds involved flow directly into other financial institutions without ever being involved in a "real" transaction (e.g., net savings bank deposits into the budget) or because, institutionally, there is no way in which they might be used to affect or disguise military procurement (e.g., the household). This does not mean, however, that some of these might not be important in the devising of financial verification systems.

After examining both budgetary and nonbudgetary sources of possible defense expenditures (Chapters 2, 3, and 4), the remainder of the book is devoted to possible methods of verification. Two approaches are proposed. The first spells out the sorts of additional economic series which would be necessary, and how some of these might be used, to detect clandestine military expenditures. The second makes use of random sampling techniques and is suggested here as an alternative because it requires fewer aggregative data from the Soviets and for this reason might be received more favorably. Neither method, unfortunately, is foolproof.

# 2

## Explicit Soviet Defense Expenditures

The problem under discussion in this paper would not exist if the Soviet budget category of defense included all state outlays of a military nature. And furthermore, the problem would be less pressing if, even though defense did not include all military outlays, the degree of inclusiveness was more precisely specified by the Soviets and the manner in which excluded military items were financed was indicated. The fact is that the Soviets present one and only one figure for military expenditures, the budgeted defense figure; and while there are some statements in the literature regarding its content, these are not quantified nor is there much discussion regarding excluded items. This vagueness also characterizes other expenditure categories in the Soviet budget, some of which might include military items.

For many reasons, it may be "natural" for a budget not to include all expenditures that might be called "military." (In fact, a first order of business in any discussion regarding limitations on military expenditures should be the definition of military expenditures.) In the United States, for example, as a result of the Atomic Energy Act, expenditures on the AEC are kept separately from those on defense, with the consequence that atomic warheads are not procured under the Department of Defense budget. Furthermore, since our federal government and its budget are separate from state and local governments and their budgets, expenditures by these latter for military purposes (say for civil defense) would not be automatically classified under national defense. Again, since almost all industry is privately owned in the U.S., investment or research and development by private enterprise to satisfy national military requirements would not be recorded as part of our defense effort (unless subsidized by the government). On the other hand, our budgeted defense figures are extremely explicit and are broken down into expenditures for thousands of individual items. Discussion of these usually occupies more than 100 pages in the U.S. federal budget. Similarly our state and local budgets are also available for public scrutiny. Finally, there is considerable information on investment by private enterprise, and major government suppliers are generally well known.

What do we know and what don't we know about the explicit defense category of the USSR State Budget? As noted above, every year the USSR budget includes an allocation to the Ministry of Defense. No detail or breakdown of this single allocation is ever given. Available Soviet sources on the budget and finance do not discuss this question in detail, and an exhaustive study of the structure of the Soviet budget by the Census Bureau found information on the formal makeup of the classification in regard to defense utterly lacking.[a] Nonetheless we do find definitions of the category in Soviet textbooks.[b] It is generally agreed that:

*Included* in the defense category are military pay and subsistence, operations and maintenance, and military construction.

*Excluded* from the defense category are military R&D, pay for border guards, and internal security (the former MVD-KGB). Probably excluded are atomic energy programs. (Obviously items such as investment in, and subsidies to, the defense industry are carried under the Financing the National Economy category of the budget, as for other branches of industry.)

*At issue* are the following:

1. Administrative outlays of the Ministry of Defense. These may be included under the budget category of administration.
2. Health facilities for the armed forces. These may be included under the budget category of health (under social-cultural outlays).
3. Education for the armed forces (military academies, etc.). Textbook definitions imply that these are included under the estimate of the Ministry of Defense, but the logic of the situation suggests they might be included under education (under social-cultural outlays).
4. Pensions. Generally they are included under the social-cultural category, but older textbooks claimed that pensions of retired officers were paid out of the defense budget.

---

[a]Gallik et al. (1968, p. 75). This source (pp. 167-181) provides the best summary in English of what is known about the explicit defense item in the Soviet Budget.

[b]For an excellent discussion of one such definition, see Becker (1964, pp. 10-12).

5. Foreign military aid. We have no idea how these outlays are financed.

6. Civil defense. Again we have no idea how this is financed.[c]

7. Procurement of major weapons. This is the most important item at issue. It is known that the defense industry pays its costs of production with revenue from sales, and thus its output must be sold to someone. Again textbook definitions usually mention procurement as an outlay of the Ministry of Defense. Suspicion surrounds this item for three reasons. First, most Western estimates of the Soviet military effort are much larger than the published explicit defense figure. Of the two major military expenses, personnel and procurement, it seems more likely that the latter "might be" excluded from the explicit defense category rather than the former. Second, according to Soviet authorities, State Material Reserves include military stocks. It is therefore tempting to assume that some part of military production is purchased not by the Ministry of Defense but as State Reserves and is thus excluded from the explicit defense category. Third, in some years (notably 1959-1960) the explicit defense allocation remained constant, at a time when Western experts were convinced that Soviet military hardware production was increasing.

---

[c]Becker (1964) cites Leon Gouré as implying that expenditures on civil defense are omitted from the defense budget and are "dispersed in the outlays of the numerous organizations and agencies . . . that oversee these activities" (p. 34).

# 3

## Other Possible Budgetary Sources of Defense Expenditure

From the preceding chapter, it seems probable that some defense expenditures are included in other parts of the State Budget. Much of the research of government economists on Soviet military expenditures has been to determine where in the budget these expenditures might be found and how much they might be. Generally speaking, it has been assumed by these persons that outright falsification, in the sense of putting the financing of military expenditures under civilian budget categories, is not practiced.[a] Procurement of tanks, for example, is not financed out of expenditures designated for paying the wages of schoolteachers. Rather, the assumption is, for example, that some investment in military plant and equipment may be financed along with other investment projects under Financing the National Economy; military R&D may come under science; and so forth. This may happen, of course, not because the Soviets are attempting to hide military expenditures, but for reasons of administrative convenience, for historical continuity, and so forth. On the other hand, this is also one of the simpler ways, though not necessarily the most effective, of hiding military expenditures.

## A. The Budget Residuals

In searching other budgetary categories for hidden defense expenditures, attention has been focused on several large and imperfectly specified residuals. There are several residuals identifiable in the Financing the National Economy category. There are also an overall budgetary expenditure residual and one connected with expenditure on science. These are the most important.

(One might ask parenthetically at this point why the Soviets have budget residuals—particularly of such large size and unknown scope. Residuals appear whenever an incompletely specified break-

---

[a]One reason for such an assumption, of course, is that if outright falsification of this sort were practiced, research on Soviet military expenditures would be almost impossible with the published data currently available to us.

down of a category is presented. The residual can be eliminated, of course, by specifying what it contains. This may not be done because the unspecified categories may be very numerous and each, taken alone, very unimportant. For a nation not given to publishing data in great detail, particularly where publication serves no operational purpose, this is an obvious reason for the existence of budget residuals. The Soviets may also use residuals to maintain secrecy in connection with receipts or expenditures which have no, or little, connection with defense. Examples are gold, currency in circulation, subsidies, and so forth. Finally, of course, the Soviets may purposely hide defense expenditures in the budget residuals.)

There are some good reasons to suspect that the residuals may, in fact, contain defense expenditures. Statements have been made in the literature on the Soviet budget that suggest this. Furthermore, large, incompletely specified residuals seem to be a logical place to hide things. In addition, their size, and the ways in which some of them have fluctuated over time, have given cause for suspicion when studied in conjunction with other independent information. Peculiarities have also been observed when the breakdown in expenditures between the Union ("federal") and Union-Republic ("state") budgets have been studied. A summary, discussion, and evaluation of the various studies made of the residuals—what we do and do not know about them—is contained in the Appendix.

No one claims, of course, that the residuals analysis provides a reliable estimate of unspecified Soviet military expenditures. It just doesn't make much sense to assume that the whole of the various residuals is "defense" when it is well known that some of them include expenditures for other items. However, perhaps for lack of other information, it has sometimes been argued that this type of analysis does provide us with a "maximum" estimate of Soviet military outlays. It has also been proposed that, even if our total military outlay figure is inaccurate, the sum of the budgeted defense figure and the "maximum" residual when viewed over time does provide us with an estimate which shows the *trend* of Soviet military spending over time.

Neither of these positions is very satisfactory. The "maximum" that any one observer comes up with is likely to differ substantially from the maximum obtained by another observer, depending on assumptions made and methods used. Furthermore, the maxima typically turn out to be very large relative to explicit defense expenditures, particularly when total defense expenditures, estimated in this fashion, are related to GNP or to other economic magnitudes.

As for the *trend* in Soviet military spending, it would obviously be very useful to have such an indicator as an unofficial monitoring device in the event of a disarmament agreement. Unfortunately, the usefulness of such a measure of trend is also questionable and for much the same reasons. We know very little about the other items included in the various residuals or their quantitative significance. Furthermore, as will be demonstrated in a later section, the Soviet regime has shown itself not particularly bound by what might be termed methodologically sound budgetary accounting conventions. Moreover, they have done considerable experimenting and reorganizing of categories. Given the large range of activities financed by the Soviet budget and the propensity for "experimentation," one must view *trends* based on the residuals analysis with considerable caution.

There are other reasons for caution in the use of the "budget residuals" approach to hidden military expenditures. If the Soviets are seriously interested in hiding their military expenditures, one wonders why they do not take more serious steps to avoid identification. They must certainly be aware by this time (if they read the *New York Times*, at least) that the various residuals are considered possible sources of military expenditures. Furthermore, since the residuals for the most part undoubtedly contain some nonmilitary expenditures, the Soviets must realize that inferences regarding military expenditures based on the residuals are apt to overstate the latter.

It would be possible for the Soviets to hide military expenditures, if they so desired, by keeping two sets of accounts: a secret set in which the items now in the residuals, including the military, are specified fully (they obviously always are specified somewhere), and a public set in which the amounts which normally would be in the residuals are spread (in some fashion) across appropriate subcategories, thereby maintaining the integrity of the total and larger subtotals albeit not of the smaller subcategories.[b] There is some reason to believe that this procedure is followed in the budget of the U.S. federal government. That is to say, expenditures for some classified projects apparently are distributed among a number of unclassified items in order to hide them.

---

[b]This would be the case if the Soviets closed out their Financing the National Economy residual by spreading the various items in it among the specified categories.

It could be argued that the above procedure does not make sense in the Soviet case. If two sets of books were being kept, why would it be necessary to hide defense expenditures under, say, science, or Financing the National Economy? Why not just leave them out of the budget? This possibility is discussed below. In the case of the United States, of course, by Article I, Section 9 of the Constitution and subsequent statutes, appropriations must be approved by Congress, must be spent for the purposes appropriated, and, therefore, must appear in the budget in an approximately appropriate place.

A second possible way of avoiding embarrassing residuals is open to the Soviets. They could presumably engage in outright falsification of category. If two sets of books were being kept, it would be just as easy to put R&D expenditures, for example, under Financing the National Economy, in the subcategory of municipal expenditures, or under Administration, as to put them under Social-Cultural Measures in the subcategory of science. For continuity, of course, this could not be done abruptly without giving rise to suspicion, and there might be limits on how much could be hidden this way.[c] There is good reason to doubt that this would be done on a very large scale: why bother to preserve the truthful identity of the whole when the parts are misrepresented? Again would it not be simpler to just set up a separate account outside of the budget for a part of defense expenditures?

Still another possibility for hiding military expenditures without residuals is to present fewer budgetary data—just present overall expenditure categories without breakdowns. (This would still leave the overall budgetary residual, which can be eliminated only by presenting one figure for budget expenditures, the total.) Thus, for example, administrative expenditures as well as defense expenditures always appear without a breakdown. In this connection, it should be noted that every time a subcategory appears in the budget without further specification, it could conceivably hide military

---

[c]It might be argued along traditional lines that the Soviets cannot conceivably keep two sets of books in the ways suggested above because of the great difficulty of maintaining consistency with interlocking economic data throughout the economy. This argument holds only if the two sets of books cover a substantial segment of the economy and if it is necessary to make available all the "interlocking economic data." If one does not have to make related data available, as the Soviets at present do not have to (and do not), then the two sets of books need only be kept in connection with a dozen or so aggregate figures presented in the budget. If, however, there were an arms control agreement, if it specified the availability of considerable related economic data, and if the stipulated expenditure reductions were not trivial, then the problems of keeping two sets of books would indeed become very substantial.

expenditures. That is to say, the reason for not presenting the further breakdown might be to avoid an embarrassing residual! (This would not appear to be a very serious possibility for most subcategories, however.)

All the above possibilities (of perhaps low probability) are presented to show some of the budgetary alternatives open to the Soviets to hide military expenditures without using residuals. They are not designed to deny that military expenditures appear in the residuals, but to suggest caution in the use of the residuals method, since other alternatives for hiding military expenditures in the budget *are* available to the Russians.

Before leaving the residuals, it should be pointed out that the work which has been done with them seems to have been confined to the 1950-1965 period. Some historical studies would appear to be in order. An attempt to analyze earlier residuals and to review trends in them might suggest different interpretations of current budgetary data. We have made here a very *casual* survey of the General Expenditures residual and the Financing the National Economy sector residual (the subcategory "other" under Financing the National Economy). Much more work, beyond our present capacity, needs to be done. We observed the trends shown in Table 3-1.

The General Expenditures residual (GER) was a decreasing percentage of total budget outlays throughout the 1930s and then again from 1950 to 1960. In the 1930s, while the General Expenditures residual was decreasing, explicit defense was increasing, as a percentage of total outlays, by great leaps. It seems obvious that the GER was not being used in the 1930s to hide military buildup. (This does not rule out the possibility, of course, that the GER included some military outlays.) The relative trends in the 1950s and 1960s perhaps need more subtle analysis. However, to the casual empiricist at least, it is noteworthy that, as mentioned, the GER residual is smaller than it was before World War II, and that the secular decline in explicit defense is accompanied by a decline in the residual—the GER even declined during the brief defense buildup in 1961-1963. Of course, the decline in the residual may reflect a decline in other nonspecified activities at the same time that more military expenditures were being included in it. This obviously requires further study.

The Financing the National Economy sector residual is much more difficult to interpret casually. We have looked at it both as a

**Table 3-1**
**Trends in Residuals and the Explicit Defense Category of the Soviet Budget, Selected Years**

| Year | Explicit Defense as Percent of Total Budget Outlay | General Expenditures Residual as Percent of Total Budget Outlay[a] | Financing the National Economy Sector Residual[b] | |
|---|---|---|---|---|
| | | | Percent of FNE | Percent of Total Budget |
| 1933 | 3 | 11 | 6 | 4 |
| 1934 | 10 | 10 | 3 | 1 |
| 1935 | 11 | 9 | 3 | 2 |
| 1936 | 16 | 7 | 7 | 3 |
| 1937 | 16 | 9 | 7 | 3 |
| 1938 | 19 | 7 | 6 | 3 |
| 1939 | 26 | 7 | 6 | 2 |
| 1940 | 33 | 8 | 10 | 3 |
| 1946 | 24 | 11 | 5 | 2 |
| 1947 | 18 | 12 | 5 | 2 |
| 1948 | 18 | 10 | 6 | 2 |
| 1949 | 19 | 10 | 10 | 4 |
| 1950 | 20 | 10 | 9 | 3 |
| 1955 | 20 | 7 | 14 | 6 |
| 1956 | 17 | 8 | 10 | 4 |
| 1957 | 15 | 6 | 11 | 5 |
| 1958 | 15 | 5 | 17 | 8 |
| 1959 | 13 | 6 | 16 | 8 |
| 1960 | 13 | 5 | 13 | 6 |
| 1961 | 15 | 5 | 8 | 3 |
| 1962 | 15 | 4 | 14 | 6 |
| 1963 | 16 | 3 | 12 | 6 |
| 1964 | 14 | 4 | 12 | 5 |
| 1965 | 13 | 4 | 17 | 8 |
| 1966 | 13 | 5 | 17 | 7 |
| 1967 | 13 | 3 | 19 | 9 |
| 1968 | 13 | 3 | 19 | 9 |
| 1969 | 13 | 3 | 19 | 8 |
| 1970 | 12 | 3 | 21 | 10 |
| 1971 | 11 | 3 | Not available | Not available |
| 1972 | 10 | 3 | | |

[a]Residual calculated in all years as total outlay less the sum of outlays to Financing the National Economy, Social-Cultural, Defense, and Administration.

[b]Residuals for 1933-1950 and 1961-1970 calculated as total Financing the National Economy less the sum of outlays to Industry, Agriculture, Trade, Procurement, Transport, Communications, and Communal Economy. For 1955-1960 outlays to Procurement are not subtracted from the total and the residual is more inclusive on this account.

Sources: K. N. Plotnikov, *Ocherki Istorii Biudzheta Sovetskogo Gosudarstva*, Moscow, 1955, p. 192-193, 206, 209, 213, 255, 261, 407, 433-434; USSR, *Gosudarstvennyi Biudzhet SSSR*, Moscow, 1962, 1966, and 1970; annual budget speeches of Minister of Finance published in *Pravda*.

percent of the total FNE category and as a percent of total budget outlay. Theoretically it seems preferable to view it as a percent of the FNE category, since in this way we are limiting our consideration to one type of activity (operating the economy) and, other things being equal, one would expect the residual to be a fairly constant percent of the total FNE category. However, we also viewed it as a percent of the total budget because, although it introduces a larger number of variables into the picture, it provides the basis for comparisons of size with explicit defense and with the General Expenditures residual.

During the 1930s, viewed as a percent of the FNE category, the residual shows a great deal of fluctuation, from 3 to 10 percent. To interpret these figures in a way which is as damaging as possible to the "residuals method," one might argue as follows. With explicit defense increasing so rapidly, it seems hard to believe that the Soviets would deliberately hide a few percentage points' worth of expenditures to give the impression of a smaller commitment. Moreover, the fluctuations in this period are often quite substantial: Why did the residual jump from 3 to 7 percent from 1935 to 1936 and from 6 percent in 1939 to 10 percent in 1940? That jumps like this occurred in periods when military expenditures were not likely to have been (fully) responsible dictates caution in reacting to current changes in them. (It should be stressed here that no attempt has been made to investigate the possible causes of the jumps mentioned.)

When the FNE residual is viewed as a percent of the total budget, it appears more stable. After an initial period of fluctuation during 1933-1935, it remained fairly constant. If military outlays were hidden here during the 1930s, they must have been small. The only question surrounds the 1933-1934 period, when the residual fell from 4 to 1 percent while defense increased from 3 to 10 percent. One might argue that in 1934, the year the Nazi regime came to power in Germany, the Russians wished to show a stronger military posture and therefore shifted some items of military significance from the residual to the explicit defense category. However, more likely, they may have curtailed some activity financed from the residual in order to concentrate more effort on defense. Or perhaps some organizational change in 1933-1934 was responsible for the decline.

Between 1946 and 1950 the residual remained at approximately the same relative size as during the 1930s, but there was a significant jump in 1949. This jump occurs whether the residual is viewed as a percent of total outlay or as a percent of FNE. Present interpretation would lean toward suspecting hidden defense outlays, but we find it hard to assume that this factor was responsible in 1949, for a number of reasons. Defense was already very large; and these years saw a rapid increase in output of consumers' goods. Since the cause in 1949 was probably not "defense," what was it? And might the same unknown factor have been responsible for other shifts? (The residual might have reflected, in some unspecified way, the large price and subsidy changes which took place in 1949.)

The 1955-1960 residuals are much larger than the earlier ones and fluctuate considerably more. The larger size is partly, but probably not entirely, due to grants to procurement agencies, which are believed to have been moderately large in some years. One might be tempted to assume that some part of the larger magnitude was due to a shift of defense expenditures into this part of the budget. This explanation, however, is hard to square with the erratic fluctuations that occurred. After 1961, the FNE residual increases steadily, except for 1963-1964, reaching a peak of 21 percent of FNE expenditures and 10 percent of the total budget in 1970. With total defense expenditures declining as a percent of the budget over this same period, it did appear for many years that the FNE residual had become a repository for clandestine military outlays. It has recently become clear, however, that subsidies to agricultural procurement agencies have been rising, and these may well account for the entire increase in the FNE residual. The reason for the increase in these subsidies is the government decision to keep retail prices of food products stable at the same time that the procurement agencies have had to pay the rural sector more for their deliveries of produce in line with the government decision to raise the incomes of that sector. The subsidies cover the resulting losses experienced by the procurement agencies. According to Krueger (1974, p. 66), subsidies were estimated at 7.9 billion rubles in 1969 and from 14.3 to 16.1 billion rubles annually in the 1970-1974 period. They amount to about 15 percent of total FNE expenditures in 1972.

## B. Other Budget Expenditure Categories

An obvious method of hiding military expenditures in the budget without showing embarrassingly large residuals is to include such expenditures within explicitly stated categories. Many explicit categories are not subdivided (e.g., the allocations to industry and to administration), and therefore the presence of military items is difficult for outside observers to detect. In some cases, the general budgetary practices of the Soviet government would appear to make this method logical. Why shouldn't military schools be financed from the allocation to education or military health services be financed from the allocation to health? Here the logic of Soviet budgetary accounting practices may reinforce a possible interest in understating the explicit defense allocation.

There are other examples. The Soviet budget allocation to administration is reported to include central government administration, outlays for running the national economy, social-cultural organizations, the Ministry of Justice, and, by implication, the Ministry of Defense (Gallik et al., 1968, pp. 75-76). The scope of military activity encompassed here can only be guessed at, but it cannot be large, since total administrative expenditures are so small. Similarly it would appear logical to include military instruction in the budget allocation to education, although here the evidence is conflicting. Some Soviet sources specifically include educational outlays under the allocation to defense, while others do not mention it in this connection. [d] A recent analysis of budget data concerning the allocation to health provides some evidence that health facilities of the armed forces may have been shifted in 1953 from the defense to the health allocation (Becker, 1964, pp. 23-24). Finally, in earlier years, pensions to retired officers were paid out of the defense budget. More recent Soviet texts are silent on this point, either because of oversight or because these pensions are not paid with Social Security funds, along with other types of pensions. Military pensions perhaps should not be considered a military expenditure.

In other cases, such accounting is less obvious. The Soviet budget annually allocates sums, under the Financing the National Economy category, for the purchase of State Reserves, i.e., for purchases of materials which are said to provide protection against unexpected crises, to supply additional resources necessary because of plan revisions, and to play an important role in increasing the defense capability (*oboronosposobnost'*) of the country (Lavrov, 1964, p. 215). State Reserves form a functional category, similar

---

[d]For examples of the former see Lavrov (1964, p. 228), or Dymshits et al. (1956, p. 223). For the latter see Allakhverdian and Liubimov (1958, p. 283) and Allakhverdian (1962, p. 310).

to investment, so that industrial reserves may be purchased[e] under the subcategory industry, agricultural reserves under the subcategory agriculture, etc., and there may be some types of purchases made under the "sector residual." There are indications that State Reserves may play an important role in the financing of defense in the Soviet Union. First, all purchases of State Reserves are made from the central All-Union Budget (1959 budget law), where one would expect sensitive military items to appear. Second, while there is no information on the size of material reserves in the budget, there is evidence that material reserves, as a national income item, are at times considerable, having amounted to as much as 5 or 6 percent of national income (Marxist style), or an estimated 6 billion rubles, in 1957.[f] It is difficult to see how these figures could have been so large unless military items were a significant factor. Unfortunately, the national income State Reserves item has not been unambiguously defined and cannot be directly related to the budgeted State Reserves item, which may include financial reserves, for example. Third, students of Soviet military expenditures have been unable to fit estimated production of military equipment into the explicit defense allocation (Godaire, 1962, p. 39), nor have they been able to explain how the defense budget remained stable (i.e., in 1959-1960) when military production was believed to be increasing. The assumption that some types of military production could have been purchased not by the Ministry of Defense but by State Reserves is a convenient explanation. This is stating a possibility, but by no means a proof.

The inclusion of military items under the budget outlay to science raises special problems. This is not directly a case of hidden military outlay, because Soviet sources openly discuss this outlay as ensuring Soviet power and prestige, especially in the missile and rocket sphere. On the other hand, inclusion of expensive research programs in this category, which has risen sharply in recent years, may well have contributed to the stability of the explicit defense allocation in, for example, the 1956-1960 period. The problem here is not only the usual one of determining how much of the allocation goes to

---

[e]If the reserves are administered centrally, they may be lumped together somewhere in the budget.

[f]Nove and Zauberman (1959, p. 198). See also discussion in Becker (1964, pp. 55-59). Casual estimates suggest that state reserves were much smaller in some other years, probably amounting to not much more than 1 billion rubles in 1959, for example.

military establishments, but in addition a basic question of the definition of military research as opposed to civilian research. Development of a rocket may be used to send a man to the moon or to send a nuclear device in attack. This is a problem to be faced in determining a workable definition of military expenditure.[g]

## C. The Budget Surplus

The Soviet budget surplus has long been suspected by naive observers (e.g., Sosnovy, 1964) as constituting a source of hidden military expenditures. Given the overall structure of the Soviet financial system, quite different from our own, it is in fact not unnatural for budget surpluses to occur in the normal course of events. In oversimplified form, the argument is as follows. Assume that a nation has two financial institutions—a budget and a bank—both of which finance an important part of the nation's nonconsumption expenditures. Assume further that the budget is the repository of all the "savings" in the economy, primarily taxes, of course; and that the bank has no independent sources of savings—its only independent source of funds is "currency creation." If it should happen that the expenditures by the bank are sufficiently large to be inflationary, then to avoid inflation, part of its expenditures would have to be financed somehow by savings from elsewhere in the economy. Since all the savings are accumulated by the budget, this is most easily accomplished, from an institutional point of view, by having the budget accumulate enough revenue over and above its own needs for financial stability and deposit this amount—its surplus—with the bank. This is essentially the Soviet picture (further details are provided later in this section and in Chapter 5, Section C). There is, however, one possible sense in which budget surpluses may be considered to indicate hidden defense expenditures: that is, if the Soviets should fail to record among their budget expenditures some payments which have been made for military purposes. In this event the recorded surplus would be spurious, at least in part. It is the opinion of the writer that it is more probable that, if expenditures are not disclosed, an equivalent amount of receipts would also be sub-

---

[g]The best source on R&D is Nimitz (1974). She estimates that between 1960 and 1968, the defense portion of R&D was about 50 percent. A recent Soviet source (Notkin, 1973) states that the science category does not include research on aerospace.

tracted from the budget, leaving the surplus unaltered. (This is discussed in Chapter 4, Section A.)

Nevertheless, the *possibility* of undisclosed expenditures resulting in budget surpluses cannot be denied, since the history of the budget surpluses contains ambiguities. For the 1930s, there are enough data to demonstrate fairly conclusively that the budget was not being manipulated in such a way as to hide expenditures and create spurious surpluses. What happens to surpluses which are realized by the budget? In the 1930s, they were deposited to the account of the budget in the Gosbank. The correspondence between realized budget surpluses and the budget account in the Gosbank was close. For example, from October 1929 through December 31, 1936, realized surpluses totaled 1.2 billion rubles. Over the same period, the budget account in the Gosbank rose from 70 million rubles to 1.13 billion, or by 1.06 billion rubles (Powell, 1952, pp. 12-13). The point of noting this correspondence between figures is that the surplus is obviously not spurious—spurious surpluses presumably would not show up in the budget account with the Gosbank.

The early postwar picture is much fuzzier. Surpluses from 1948 (after the currency reform) to 1950 totaled 7.4 billion rubles and those from 1951 to 1956 were reported as totaling 14.1 billion rubles. The only figure for budget deposits in this period is for January 1, 1956: approximately 8.0 billion rubles.[h] Clearly some other disposition must have been made of the accrued surpluses.

This problem can be looked at in another way. As noted above, the budget surpluses are often viewed as a means of financing the short-term (working capital) lending activities of the Gosbank. In fact, to the extent that the deposits of the budget in the Gosbank fall short of the increase in short-term loans, new (net) deposits must be created or new (net) notes must be added to currency in circulation (ignoring minor items). So, for example, on January 1, 1937, the asset side of the Gosbank balance sheet showed short-term loans of almost 3.5 billion rubles and the liability side showed the following: budget deposits, 1.13 billion; other enterprise deposits, 1.19 billion; note issue, 1.08 billion. The budget deposits here, of course, correspond closely to the budget surpluses reported.

Now, as noted above, budget surpluses for 1948-1956 totaled 21.5 billion rubles, while the increase in short-term credit extended

[h]V. K. Sitnin has stated that budget accounts were equal to "about 40 percent" of bank loans, which at the time were 19.4 billion rubles. See Sitnin (1956, p. 56).

over the period totaled much less—15.8 billion rubles (24.4 − 8.6). The interesting question is: What happened to the budget surpluses of the earlier postwar period? Obviously, if these funds had been completely immobilized, they would have constituted a substantial "deflationary" force. [i] This gives rise to the suspicion, and there is evidence to support it, that part, at least, of the surpluses was spurious and/or expended in irregular ways.

First, there appears to be at least one source of spurious surpluses, or what in effect involves double-count. Apparently, unexpended funds of local institutions and organizations, as well as local budget surpluses, are regarded as revenue in the subsequent year (Gallik et al., 1968, p. 63; see Division 16).

Second, some of the surpluses have regularly been deposited to the credit of the long-term investment banks, now to the Stroibank. This may also have been the case in the period in question.

Third, during part of the early 1950s, and perhaps during the whole 1948-1955 period, the budget financed certain types of additions to working capital not out of current revenue, as normal additions to working capital are financed, but out of accumulated surpluses. [j] These were very special working capital requirements, however, having been generated by the series of substantial price cuts effected from 1948 to 1954. That is to say, the value of stocks held by enterprises was reduced by the price cuts, thus inflicting capital losses on the enterprises. The loss in 1954 was, according to Nove, some 650 million rubles. The losses in earlier years when the price cuts were much larger must have been commensurately greater.

If the working capital grants had been made by extension of additional short-term credit—this would, of course, be an unusual

---

[i] There were, of course, substantial reductions in prices over the 1948-1956 period. Nevertheless, these reductions were not sufficient to have required a decline in either cash or deposit currency (as immobilization of part of the budget surplus would have implied). This is deduced from the fact that wages and the numbers of workers in the labor force increased steadily over the whole period. Furthermore, casual empiricism suggests that the increase in volume of goods produced and sold was greater than the decline in prices over the period in question, implying that the need for "means of payment" was increasing (unless it was being used more efficiently—that is, unless velocity of circulation was increasing).

[j] See Powell (1962), Nove (1954, pp. 415-424), Kisman and Slavnyi (1956, pp. 26, 32, 33). Nove feels that this was not done until 1954. Kisman and Slavnyi, which is a later Russian source than was available to Nove, suggest that it was done earlier as well. Nove also argues that the expenditures were made by the creation of "spurious" receipts as in the case of gains to the consumers, but this seems not to have been the case—nor could it have been, since these are real transfers.

way of compensating enterprises for capital losses—the result would have been a larger short-term loan figure and a larger budget deposit figure. Or if the working capital had been granted out of current budget receipts, the result would have been a smaller budget deposit figure, but also a smaller current surplus. In either event, the budgetary anomalies referred to above would have been reduced. What appears to have happened is that Gosbank loans were less than they might have been, the budget deposit account was less, and the current surpluses were large. The Soviets, in effect, drew down the budget account in the Gosbank to finance current working capital expenditures. This is, it should be noted, the reverse of taking accounts out of the budget to hide them. It involves putting into the budget transactions which might have been kept out.

It is impossible to say whether these possible explanations of the early postwar budget surpluses are exhaustive. But it hardly seems likely. The reused surpluses and the deposits to the credit of the long-term investment banks were undoubtedly small. It is possible, however, that financing the losses in working capital of enterprises could have made up the remainder; our limited exploration of this question does not allow us to come to a conclusion.

There are two further important possible explanations of the relatively small budget deposit account in the face of such large surpluses. First, over the years 1941-1943, the budget ran actual deficits, the only one in its history (Holzman, 1955, Chapter 9). These totaled about 4.0 billion rubles, and must have put the budget in debt to Gosbank to the tune of some 2.0 to 2.5 billion rubles (since the budget's deposits must have totaled about 1.5 to 2.0 billion rubles on the eve of the war). While this may explain in part the smallness of the budget deposit account, it does not contribute to our understanding of the large size of the budget surpluses relative to the short-term loans of the Gosbank and the shortage of currency this presumably should have created in the economy.

A final possibility to explain the small budget figure, but again not an explanation of the high budget surplus/Gosbank loan ratio, is that the budget deposits were used up in some capital transaction. We know, for example, that the budget deposit account was reduced in 1939 by some .6 billion rubles to retire Government bonds issued in the early 1930s (Powell, 1952). It is possible that a similar transaction was performed after the Currency Reform of 1947. At that time, some 5 to 10 billion rubles' worth of paper currency was called in from circulation and exchanged for new notes at a ratio of 10 for 1 (Holzman, 1955, Chapter 9). This would have left the Gosbank with a capital gain of from, say, 4.5 to 9.0 billion rubles. Perhaps the budget surpluses of the 1948-1956 period were devoted in part to canceling these notes. We still must explain, however, how the economy would sustain such currency-reducing transactions.[k]

The picture in recent years is clouded by the fact that there are no firm figures on the budget deposit account in the Gosbank after 1956. This precludes any attempt to verify the validity of the budget surplus figure by examining changes in the budget's account in the Gosbank. On the other hand, the relationship between the budget surplus and the increase in short-term lending of the Gosbank is more "normal." From 1958 through 1973, surpluses totaled approximately 20 billion rubles, whereas the increase in short-term credit extended amounted to a little over 70 billion rubles.[l] Whereas before, we were hard put to explain what could have happened to the large surpluses realized by the budget and some observers might have suspected their expenditure for clandestine military purposes, the present situation does not lend itself to any such interpretation.

## D. Industrial Subsidies and the Meaning of Prices

The budgets of most nations contain subsidies which finance the losses of enterprises or organizations. (Agricultural subsidies were discussed in Section A of this chapter.) The losses may be due to the inability of the enterprise to operate profitably at competitive prices or may be due to a decision to keep the prices of some goods or services at below-cost for social reasons. The Soviet budget has always included industrial subsidies and these have often (especially before 1948) been very large, as a result of the decision to keep the prices of producers' goods and raw materials relatively stable in the face of rising costs. These subsidies have usually been included in

[k]A possible (but highly unlikely, in my opinion) explanation is that substantial repressed inflation still existed after the Currency Reform and the large budget surpluses were required to complete the job left unfinished by the Reform. The relatively low level of collective farm market prices in the 1948-1950 period, however, suggests a very low level of repressed inflation. See Holzman (1960, pp. 168-169).

[l]The gap between the two figures must be bridged by deposits of other enterprises and organizations and by expansion of currency in circulation (see Table 1-1). The best and most recent source on monetary statistics of the USSR is Powell (1967).

the Financing the National Economy category along with investment in fixed and working capital and several other minor classes of expenditures (see Tables A-1 and A-2 in the Appendix). The Russians have, with a few postwar exceptions, not disclosed the amounts of subsidies contained in the annual budgets. Furthermore, the subsidies have not been broken down by destination, i.e., by product or branch of industry. (In addition, subsidies are not "gross" because profits of some enterprises have been used to cover losses by other enterprises in the same industry. From our point of view, however, this is not significant.)

The problem with subsidies is not that the Soviets include them among their budget expenditures. They should be included; otherwise the real size of the overall budget would be less than it should be, since the subsidies represent below-cost prices. The problem is that while the validity of the aggregate budget is maintained by the subsidies, the distribution of expenditures is distorted. Thus, suppose a tank factory is selling tanks to the Ministry of Defense for 200,000 rubles, the true cost of a tank. This expenditure would show up under defense as 200,000 rubles. Suppose the tanks were subsidized to sell for 100,000 rubles each. The budget expenditure would still be 200,000 rubles of which, however, 100,000 would be subsidy to the tank enterprise through Financing the National Economy and 100,000 would be defense. The net result of this procedure would be to understate defense in the budget. The well-known general use of the subsidy procedure in the past raises questions regarding the interpretation of past defense expenditures in the budget and raises the possibility that it might be deliberately used in the future to mask the true extent of the military effort.

### E. Pricing Problems

Pricing problems have already been touched on in connection with subsidies and will be touched on again in connection with retained profits. The discussion here applies not only to the budget but also to the assessment of expenditures made by enterprises or institutions. There are actually several pricing problems that must be faced in any comparison of the military strengths of different nations, and some of these are more crucial to the problem of mutual armament reduction than others.

First, there is the unavoidable problem that factor scarcities differ between nations, in this case the USSR and the U.S. Thus the cost of technicians may be relatively less, of missiles relatively more, in the Soviet Union than in the United States. Under these circumstances, comparisons of military strength lead unavoidably to ambiguities usually classified under the heading of index-number problems.

Second, to the problems caused by these "natural" price differences can be added the peculiarities of Soviet pricing. On the one hand, Soviet prices differ from Western prices in that they do not include comparable charges for capital, land, or entrepreneurial services, nor are they sensitive to the degree of excess (deficient) demand; on the other hand, prices often further deviate from cost as a result of the extensive use of subsidies and sales taxes. These factors seriously complicate any attempt to compare the "real" military effort of the two nations at a given point of time.

What problems, if any, do these create for a mutual arms reduction agreement couched in financial terms? There are basically two problems.

First, in an agreement to reduce budget military expenditures of the sort envisioned, no specification is to be made regarding the types of items to be reduced. Given an agreement to reduce expenditures by, say, 20 percent, a nation might concentrate the entire reduction in manpower, or perhaps in aircraft, or perhaps all subgroups of military expenditures might be reduced proportionally. (Undoubtedly there will be real restraints on the "reduction mix." Thus it would not make much sense to reduce personnel without reducing the food purchased to feed them; or to eliminate an airbase without cutting back on the personnel connected with the airbase.) As long as the prices of the items cut back represent the "real" costs of these items to the nations concerned, then it shouldn't matter what the particular "reduction mix" is. In effect, the resources devoted to defense by the two nations will have been reduced by the same percentage.[m] (That one nation may lose military power relative to another by a given percentage reduction of military expendi-

---

[m]For the usual index-number reasons, the way the mixes are chosen may make either nation feel that it has gained or lost by the operation.

tures is another question.) On the other hand, if prices do not represent real costs because of sales taxes[n] or subsidies or other pricing quirks, then a given percentage reduction in military expenditures may represent a different commitment of resources in different countries. Thus, if the cutback is heavily concentrated on subsidized items, the degree of disarmament is larger in real than in financial terms; if concentrated on items carrying heavy sales taxes, the degree of disarmament is smaller in real than in financial terms. Suppose, for example, that the military budget is spent one-half on manpower and one-half on food and other subsistence. Suppose further that the sales tax on food and other subsistence purchased by the Ministry of Defense is 100 percent. Suppose finally that a 20 percent cutback in military expenditures is concentrated 10 percent on manpower expenditures and 10 percent on food and other subsistence expenditures. In this event, the real resource cutback would be equal to the financial cutback, or 20 percent. On the other hand, if the entire cutback were in food and subsistence, the real cutback would be only 13 $\frac{1}{3}$ percent. If the entire cutback were in men, the real cutback would be 26 $\frac{2}{3}$ percent. If food and other subsistence were subsidized, the results would be just the reverse. It seems clear that the existence of subsidies and sales taxes creates incentives to bias cutbacks in the direction of commodities with sales taxes and away from commodities which are subsidized. (This is just another case of the traditional "success indicator.")

Second, an agreement to reduce military expenditures by a given percentage will have comparable significance in real terms only if prices remain unchanged. Thus military expenditures can be reduced by 20 percent by simply reducing prices 20 percent, leaving quantities unchanged. Should it be desired to avoid reducing real military expenditures in the face of an agreement to reduce budgeted defense expenditures, there would no doubt be an incentive to effect the reduction in part by subsidizing the prices of some material or reducing sales taxes on others. The subsidies would, of course, still be in the budget (unless they were financed out of retained profits, as will be indicated later), but presumably they would remain unspecified. The elimination of sales taxes would reduce turnover tax revenue, but again for unspecified reasons.

[n]In some instances, e.g., petroleum and copper, the turnover tax does represent, at least in part, real costs which are otherwise omitted because of the Marxian approach to costing, particularly before the 1965 reform.

One methodological obstacle to dealing with this problem is that prices might decline because of productivity increases rather than as a result of tax and subsidy manipulations. This could happen quite dramatically in the military field because of the rapidity of technological change and the relative speed with which products once developed are put into large-scale production. Suppose a nation has a rapid increase in productivity in the production of military equipment and this is reflected in a price decline. Should the resource commitment be measured in terms of factors committed to production, which remain constant, or in terms of the amount of equipment produced, which increases? (It would seem to me to be preferable, and certainly less ambiguous , to couch arms reduction agreements in terms of outputs rather than inputs.)

## F. Unconventional Budget Accounting Practices

The extent to which the Soviet administrators are free to manipulate budget accounts to their own ends was demonstrated in the early 1950s in connection with the price changes which occurred at that time. Some of these were mentioned earlier in connection with the budget surplus and need not be repeated in detail here.[o] In the late 1940s and early 1950s, the Soviet government regularly reduced prices, particularly those of consumers' goods. In addition, in the 1950s, procurement prices of agricultural products were raised several times.

The decline in consumers' goods prices was effected largely by reducing the percentage of turnover tax in price. This was reflected in the budget from 1948 through 1952 as a relatively small increase (compared to what might have been) in revenue from the turnover tax. In 1953, according to Nove, the practice was changed. The price cuts of April of that year, which presumably saved the consumer some 4.3 billion rubles, were included on both sides of the budget: on the receipts side in Other Revenue as "sums devoted to the reduction of retail prices," and in Other Expenditure as a "sum devoted to

---

[o]We refer to two budgetary operations: first, the granting of funds in the 1950s to enterprises, to compensate them for working capital losses sustained as a result of price cuts, by drawing down the budget deposit in the Gosbank rather than out of current revenues; second, the retirement in 1939 of .6 billion rubles' worth of bonds issued during the Credit Reform, also by drawing down the budget account in the Gosbank.

reducing consumers' goods prices.''[p] This process was repeated in the 1954 price reduction. The addition of these items to the aggregate budget residuals (and the ability to add similar transactions in the future) certainly confuses the significance one might attach to these residuals in connection with military expenditures. It also tends to affect the meaning in "real" terms that one can attribute to the money value of the total budget.

In 1954, procurement prices of agricultural products were raised by 2.3 billion rubles without change in retail prices. Proper methodology would have shown this as an increase in expenditures by procurement agencies to peasants (not in budget) of 2.3 billion rubles which is financed, in effect, by a reduction in turnover tax receipts of like amount. In fact, payments by the procurement agencies to agricultural producers did go up by 2.3 billion rubles. However, the procurement agencies kept the old low price on their books, thereby, in effect, taking a planned loss (selling at a lower price than they had bought) and also leaving the revenue side of the budget unchanged. That is to say, the revenue side of the budget was spuriously inflated by 2.3 billion rubles. These 2.3 billion rubles were then disbursed as subsidies to the procurement agencies to cover their planned losses. In subsequent years, when the books of the procurement agencies were altered to show the true price of their payments to the agricultural producers, the spurious revenue item was eliminated, as was the subsidy to the procurement agency.[q] It is not clear how the agricultural subsidies of the late 1960s and 1970s are being handled (Krueger, 1974, p. 64).

---

[p]For details of this and the following procedures, see Nove (1954, pp. 415-424). Also see U.S., CIA, *The 1960 Soviet Budget*; and Kisman and Slavnyi (1956, pp. 26, 32, 33).

[q]Abraham Becker has informed me that subsidies to procurement persisted, though on a diminishing scale, through 1962.

# 4

## Possible Nonbudgetary Sources of Military Expenditures

A number of other possible sources of military expenditures are examined in this chapter. While most of them do not appear very likely candidates, they are presented to make the financial picture as complete as possible.

### A. Separate Secret Accounts Outside the Budget

Perhaps the simplest technique of hiding expenditures from public view is to set up separate accounts outside of the State Budget. Separate accounts already exist in many countries, although these are not usually for the purpose of hiding things but exist as a matter of administrative convenience or for accidental historical reasons. In the United States, for example, federally financed highways are not included in the administrative budget but are financed largely out of trust funds of the Department of Commerce, which funds are obtained from taxes on highway users. Similarly, most of the expenditures under the Federal National Mortgage Association (Fanny May) are handled outside the budget as trust funds. In many countries, military expenditures have been made by local governments or governments of territories (colonies) and have not appeared in federal budgets (League of Nations, 1933-1935, Vol. 1, pp. 80-83). These can be viewed, in effect, as separate accounts. (The Soviet practice, mentioned in Chapter 3, of drawing down the budget deposit account in the Gosbank to retire government bonds might be considered a use of the "separate account" technique, since it by-passes the regular budget.)

The separate account technique is an extremely flexible instrument and can be introduced at any time, not only to encompass the financing of whole categories of expenditures but for any portion of a category that it is deemed desirable to hide. One failing of the system derives from the fact that, normally, one would probably want to subtract from the regular budget both the receipts and expenditures sides of the hidden expenditure. However, most of the receipts of a budget are usually rather formally structured and the subtraction of a part of them would, in theory at least, be subject to fiscal verification.

If just military expenditures were removed from the budget, as discussed in Chapter 3, a spurious surplus would result. If the surplus were deposited in the Gosbank, presumably it would then be spent through the Gosbank on military goods. Furthermore, as noted earlier, it would undoubtedly be reported as a loan even though it would be a grant.

It is also possible that that part of the surplus which represents hidden military expenditures may not be deposited in the Gosbank[a] but simply held in some unspecified fashion until spent. This would be the equivalent of setting up a separate secret account. The problem of verification would appear to be somewhat more difficult if just expenditures are removed from the budget because of the absence of a possible "receipts" check. Under these circumstances, one would need not only data on budget receipts but information on the whole financial system, particularly the banking system.

There is no information, to my knowledge, on whether or not the Soviets keep secret accounts. Certainly, their centralized public finance system excludes the possibility that military expenditures could be hidden in the legitimate budgets of local authorities. On the other hand, any number of alternative separate accounts have been and are available for use. The possible use of secret accounts would seem to pose serious problems of verification in the event of an agreement for mutual reduction of military expenditures.

## B. Bank Credit

The State Bank or Gosbank is the source of about 90 percent of the credit granted in the Soviet Union, and 90 percent of the credit granted by that institution is for short-term working capital purposes. The remaining 10 percent of Gosbank loans are long-term and are extended to farms, cooperatives, and individuals. The Investment (Construction) Bank, or Stroibank, is responsible for roughly

---

[a]We have seen that the correspondence between budget surpluses and the budget deposit account in the Gosbank has been "weak" in the postwar period.

10 percent of the credits outstanding in the economy; two-thirds of these are for long-term investments, the remainder for short-term working capital needs. (These various percentages are for January 1, 1969; see Gerashchenko, 1970.) Until 1965, both the loans by the Investment Bank and long-term loans by both banks were trivial in amount. Since then, as a result of the Economic Reform, an increasing percentage of long-term investment has been funded through the banks on a credit basis rather than as a direct budget expenditure[b] or from retained funds of enterprises. However, new financing from this source still amounts to less than 2 percent of expenditures on the national economy (see Table 4-5) and no more than 5 percent of gross investment. Tables 4-1 and 4-2 show total loans outstanding, and short-term loans categorized by sector of the economy and by type of credit for selected years.

Data are provided annually in the statistical handbooks showing changes in short-term credit outstanding by branch and by purpose. The data are presented more comprehensively than those of the budget in the sense that residuals are very small. The annual increments to loans outstanding occasionally show some disconcerting jumps (e.g., the increase from 1958 to 1959—not shown here—is about twice as large as that for any nearby year), but there is no reason to suspect that this was due to the use of the Bank for purposes other than formally authorized. (Fluctuations in the 1930s were also erratic, but largely explicable on nonmilitary grounds; see Powell, 1952.)

It is possible, however, that some expenditures which might be classified as "military" are contained in the Bank's figures. For example, it seems probable that some part of the expansion of short-term credit to industry and construction may represent an increase in working capital loans to industries producing military goods. This would be the counterpart in this country of Boeing obtaining a working capital loan from a private bank: it would represent, in effect, part of the U.S. real military expenditures for the year. How large are such expenditures likely to have been? Probably not very large. While the increase in short-term loans has averaged, say, 4 to 5 billion rubles a year, which is a substantial amount, most of this certainly is required to meet the legitimate

---

[b]Actually, the increase in loans by the Stroibank each year is financed indirectly by grants from the budget (Gerashchenko, 1970).

**Table 4-1**
**Bank Credits to the National Economy and to the Population, Selected Years (loans outstanding at the end of the year; in billions of rubles)**

| | 1952 | 1958 | 1965 | 1970 | 1971 | 1972 |
|---|---|---|---|---|---|---|
| Short-term credits: total | 21.436 | 33.153 | 68.012 | 108.175 | 115.394 | 120.859 |
| Industry | 8.285 | 13.184 | 23.567 | 35.467 | 37.216 | 37.732 |
| Agriculture | .547 | 1.506 | 4.636 | 9.457 | 17.017 | 14.027 |
| Transport and communication | .225 | .276 | .592 | 1.368 | 1.478 | 1.194 |
| Construction | 1.057 | 1.067 | 3.452 | 8.830 | 8.932 | 10.502 |
| Supply | 2.404 | 4.030 | 4.354 | 8.482 | 8.546 | 9.105 |
| Procurement | 1.021 | 1.718 | 5.281 | 8.388 | 7.688 | 8.189 |
| Trade | 7.628 | 11.228 | 25.698 | 35.125 | 38.582 | 39.279 |
| Other | .269 | .144 | .432 | 1.058 | .935 | .831 |
| Long-term credits: total | 2.252 | 3.984 | 6.018 | 18.059 | 21.635 | 29.682 |
| Collective farms | .997 | 2.173 | 3.890 | 10.296 | 11.639 | 13.458 |
| Population | .638 | .828 | .809 | .646 | .617 | .608 |
| State and cooperative enterprises and Organizations | .617 | .983 | 1.319 | 7.117 | 9.379 | 15.616 |

Source: USSR, Tsentral'noe Statisticheskoe Upravlenie, *Narodnoe Khoziaistvo SSSR v 1962 g.*, Moscow 1963, p. 639; USSR, Tsentral'noe Statisticheskoe Upravlenie, *Narodnoe Khoziaistvo SSSR v 1972 g.*, Moscow 1973, p. 728.

Table 4-2
**Short-Term Bank Credits to the National Economy by Type of Credit, Selected Years (loans outstanding at the end of the year; in billions of rubles)**

| | 1952 | 1958 | 1965 | 1970 | 1971 | 1972 |
|---|---|---|---|---|---|---|
| Short-term credits: total | 21.436 | 33.153 | 68.012 | 108.175 | 115.394 | 120.859 |
| Loans with commodity collateral | 13.921 | 24.669 | 51.092 | 83.080 | 87.357 | 91.945 |
| Stocks of production materials | 2.867 | 7.498 | 13.287 | 24.434 | 26.299 | 28.150 |
| Unfinished production | .763 | .682 | 1.489 | 2.146 | 1.936 | 1.580 |
| Finished goods | .709 | 1.766 | 3.448 | 3.570 | 3.203 | 3.295 |
| Equipment stocks in construction | .287 | .527 | 1.140 | 2.888 | 2.687 | 2.864 |
| Goods: | | | | | | |
| In retail trade | 6.646 | 9.538 | 21.139 | 28.755 | 31.508 | 31.844 |
| With supply organizations | 1.335 | 2.145 | 2.347 | 5.306 | 5.199 | 5.628 |
| With procurement organizations | .577 | 1.271 | 4.353 | 7.441 | 6.725 | 7.052 |
| Other commodity collateral | .423 | .488 | 1.693 | 3.728 | 5.025 | 6.548 |
| Loans under account (settlement documents in process, etc.) | 5.955 | 6.857 | 12.141 | 16.501 | 17.975 | 19.748 |
| Other | 1.560 | 1.627 | 4.779 | 8.594 | 10.062 | 9.166 |

Source: USSR, Tsentral'noe Statisticheskoe Upravlenie, *Narodnoe Khoziaistvo SSSR v 1962 g.*, Moscow 1963, p. 640; USSR, Tsentral'noe Statisticheskoe Upravlenie, *Narodnoe Khoziastvo SSSR v 1972 g.*, Moscow 1973, p. 729.

working capital requirements of nonmilitary industry. This presumably would not leave much funds for military expenditures.[c]

The question may be asked: In the event of an agreement to reduce budgeted military expenditures, could short-term loans by the Gosbank be used as a substitute? Presumably they could, although there is no reason to believe that the Gosbank method would in any way be more appropriate than setting up a secret account outside the budget or than spreading the amounts in question around into other items in the budget. In fact, the Gosbank way would seem much less appropriate in view of the facts that (a) the Gosbank is primarily an institution for granting short-term credit; (b) according to Powell (1952), Gosbank loan policy has always been applied very formalistically; and (c) in contrast, as noted above, the budget has on numerous occasions been the victim of unorthodox accounting practices.

If the Gosbank were used as a subterfuge, it would have to finance military expenditures as donations, rather than as loans, although the grants would no doubt appear in the accounts as loans. Presumably, they would be financed (in effect) by the budget revenues deposited as part of the budget surplus in the Gosbank. The government would certainly not reduce taxes and finance these expenditures by net currency (deposit or note) creation, since this would tend to be inflationary.

To conclude in a cautionary mood, however, it should be noted that although the total loans outstanding each year (with breakdowns) have been published, as have the sums of the deposit accounts of enterprises, the overall balance sheet of the Gosbank has not been published in the postwar period and there has been an almost complete blackout on note issue, budget deposits, and numerous miscellaneous items. Absence of such data would make it difficult to detect any attempt by the government (unlikely as it appears) to use the Gosbank to hide military expenditures under short-term credits.

The recent increase in long-term credits, particularly to state and cooperative enterprises and organizations (see Table 4-1), by the Gosbank and Stroibank as a result of the attempt to decentralize

---

[c]The smallness of possible unexplicitly recorded working capital loans to military industry is underlined by Stanley Cohn's (1962, p. 72) figures which show total inventory investment in 1960 in the USSR at 1.3 percent of GNP, in comparison with gross capital investment of 31.3 percent and estimated defense of 10.2 percent.

investment under the economic reforms, opens up another possible avenue for clandestine financing of military expenditures. Although currently of much smaller magnitude than short-term loans, and for this reason not as convenient a "hiding place," the long-term credits are nevertheless a more natural receptacle for such expenditures, particularly if these should be investment expenditures. Because of the lack of data on the balance sheets of both the Gosbank and the Stroibank, use of long-term loans for such purposes would be very difficult to detect. Should there continue to be sharp increases in investment from these sources, one might investigate trends in other sources of investment and in total investment for suspicious deviations. In the case of the Stroibank, it is worth noting that the organization cannot create credit like the Gosbank but finances investment either from repayments on previous lendings or from new donations from the State Budget. To the extent that these donations do not represent the deposit of the budget surplus but are contained somewhere in one of the budget expenditure categories, it is important to avoid double-counting the increment to investment, whether it be for military or other purposes.

To conclude, the possibility that military expenditures could be financed through the long-term credit apparatus of the Gosbank and Stroibank cannot be completely discounted and would be very difficult to verify.

## C. Retained Profits of Enterprises

A major source of funds which do not go through the budget is the retained profits of state enterprises. In recent years, about three-fifths of total profits earned by state enterprises have been deducted into the budget, the remainder having been left to the disposal of the enterprise (see Tables 4-4 and 4-5). The percentages of both total profits (Table 4-3) and retained profits as sources of finance have tended to increase over the years.

The major uses of retained profits are for investment in fixed and working capital and in the formation of enterprise incentive funds. Both of these uses have been on the increase as a result of the economic reforms. In addition, retained profits have had several minor uses such as repayment of Gosbank loans, financing planned losses of other enterprises, and the like. Since retained profits were

**Table 4-3**
**Profits in the National Economy of the USSR, Selected Years (billions of rubles)**

| | 1952 | 1958 | 1965 | 1970 | 1971 | 1972 |
|---|---|---|---|---|---|---|
| Total profits | 7.299 | 20.112 | 36.960 | 86.989 | 90.148 | 93.445 |
| Profit of state enterprises | 6.922 | 19.303 | 36.062 | 85.668 | 88.510 | 91.691 |
| Industry | 3.772 | 10.677 | 22.548 | 55.956 | 56.232 | 59.397 |
| Agriculture and procurement | – .186 | .515 | .100 | 6.117 | 5.921 | 3.739 |
| Transport and communication | 1.468 | 3.507 | 6.830 | 11.523 | 12.207 | 12.626 |
| Construction | – .246 | .818 | 1.605 | 4.736 | 5.571 | 6.249 |
| Supply | .355 | .897 | .892 | 1.696 | 2.159 | 2.547 |
| Trade | .638 | 1.300 | 1.398 | 2.859 | 3.023 | 3.561 |
| Communal economy | .261 | .491 | .748 | .984 | 1.234 | 1.270 |
| Other | .860 | 1.098 | 1.941 | 1.797 | 2.163 | 2.302 |
| Profit of consumer cooperatives | .377 | .809 | .898 | 1.321 | 1.638 | 1.754 |

Source: Tsentral'noe Statisticheskoe Upravlenie, *Narodnoe Khoziaistvo SSSR v 1962 g.*, Moscow 1963, p. 627; USSR, Tsentral'noe Statisticheskoe Upravlenie, *Narodnoe Khoziaistvo SSSR v 1972 g.*, Moscow 1973, p. 697.

## Table 4-4
## Use of Profits of State Enterprises and Economic Organizations (percent)

|  | 1965 | 1968 | 1970 | 1971 | 1972 |
|---|---|---|---|---|---|
| Total profits received | 100 | 100 | 100 | 100 | 100 |
| Paid to budget | 71 | 67 | 62 | 62 | 60 |
| Retained | 29 | 33 | 38 | 38 | 40 |
| Used for: |  |  |  |  |  |
| Capital investment | 9 | 10 | 14 | 13 | 13 |
| Enterprise incentive funds | 6 | 12 | 14 | 14 | 16 |

Source: USSR, Tsentral'noe Statisticheskoe Upravlenie, *Narodnoe Khoziaistvo SSSR v 1972 g.*, Moscow 1973, p. 698; *Narodnoe Khoziaistvo SSSR, 1922-1972*, Moscow 1972, p. 466.

## Table 4-5
## Financing the National Economy of the USSR—Plan 1972 (billions of new rubles)

| Branch | Budget Funds | Own Funds[a] | Bank Credit | Total |
|---|---|---|---|---|
| Industry and construction | 32.0 | 53.7 | 1.3 | 87.0 |
| Agriculture and procurement | 12.1 | 14.3 | 1.2 | 27.6 |
| Transport and communications | 3.2 | 11.3 | — | 14.5 |
| Communal and housing | 5.6 | 1.0 | — | 6.6 |
| Other | 29.7 | 4.3 | 0.1 | 34.1 |
| Total | 82.6 | 84.6 | 2.6 | 169.8 |

[a]Own funds consist primarily of retained profit and amortization deductions, but also include minor items such as economies from reductions in construction costs. Retained profits were planned at 40.4 billion rubles in 1972. In 1972, amortization deductions totaled 35.3 billion rubles, of which 17.8 billion rubles were used for repair.

Source: *Finansy SSSR*, No. 1, 1972, p. 6

planned at roughly 40.4 billion rubles in 1972, roughly 13 billion rubles will be channeled into new investment (see Tables 4-4 and 4-5).

We know that the profit figures published by the USSR are netted to some extent, but it is impossible to tell by how much. Profits may be distributed within an enterprise from commodities which are produced at a profit to others which are sold at a loss. Similarly, the ministries have the right to redistribute funds from profitable enterprises to those operating at a loss. (This was recently corroborated in *Finansy SSSR*, Vol. 1, 1974, p. 5.) On the other hand, profits are gross to the extent that the budget still[d] subsidizes the losses of some enterprises.

While there are no significant or suspicious residuals in the disposition of retained profits, in other respects they pose much the same kinds of problems as budget expenditures in general. It is certainly possible that part of investment in fixed and working capital from retained profits could be in industries related to the military.

Even more elusive is the case in which profits may be transferred among enterprises in the same ministry or among products in the same enterprise. There are at least two possible ways in which military expenditures might be hidden through such transfers. First, profits of nonmilitary products or enterprises may be used to cover losses, that is to say, below-cost prices of military products. If this were done, defense expenditures would be reduced by the amount of the subsidy. Second, the profits of nonmilitary products or enterprises could conceivably be diverted to financing investment in military products in the same or other enterprises without the usual mediation of the budget. Finally, the profits of enterprises could be used to procure military hardware which is then delivered without charge to the Ministry of Defense. In other words, the budget would receive military hardware from enterprises in place of deductions from profits.

There is no particular reason to assume that any one of these possibilities is realized in practice at all or on a significant scale. However, they are possible practices. To the extent that enterprises or ministries produce a mix of military and nonmilitary products, the transfer of funds remains a possible subterfuge in the event of an agreement to mutually reduce budgeted military expenditures.

## D. Amortization (Depreciation) Funds

Along with retained profits, enterprises have available to them amortization or depreciation funds, which are accumulated in much the same way as in capitalist countries. At present, these are the two

---

[d]Presumably industrial subsidies were largely eliminated by the early 1950s. A 1964 source made it clear that the budget still paid enterprises for planned losses (Lavrov, 1964, p. 217). Although the 1967 price reform eliminated most industrial subsidies again, it would be surprising if some subsidies were still not being financed through the budget.

major sources of enterprise "own" funds and are of roughly equal importance. From Table 4-5 it can be seen that "own" funds of enterprises finance as large a part of Financing the National Economy as do budgeted funds.

In a sense, what has been said of retained profits may be repeated here for the amortization funds. These funds may be used for replacement of equipment and, in contradistinction to capitalist practice, for capital repairs as well. To the extent that they are used to replace or repair equipment in plants producing military items by more than is charged to cost in such plants, and do not go through budgeted defense, the latter item may be considered to be understated. Although amortization funds are as sizable as retained profits, it seems even more unlikely that they would either normally—or surreptitiously—represent hidden military expenditures of any sizable amount. First, under normal circumstances, that part of the amortization funds which is charged to military industries is bound to be small because the capital stock of military industries is likely to be small relative to that for all industry. Second, amortization deductions in the Soviet Union are generally considered to substantially understate Soviet replacement requirements. The percentage that depreciation (amortization) is of GNP in the USSR has typically been about half that in the U.S.—and half of the Soviet figure reflects capital repair (Campbell, 1963, Chapter 4). It seems unlikely, therefore, that amortization or repair funds generated in the accounts of nonmilitary enterprises would be diverted to military purposes. If they were, replacement investment and repair of nonmilitary plant and equipment would have to come from other sources. Third, it seems even more unlikely in the case of amortization funds than of retained profits that the former funds would be used to subsidize below-cost prices of military equipment.

Despite all these caveats, all "own" funds, including those from amortization deductions, could be used to mask the true destination of investment in military plant and equipment; and certainly a small amount of gross military investment is effected (as indicated earlier) in the spending of these funds.


## E. Deductions from Enterprise Costs of Production

Outlays charged to the enterprise costs of production (*sebestoi-*

*most'*) may constitute an additional nonbudget source of financing military outlays, albeit a small one. Ordinarily items charged to *sebestoimost'* are reflected in the cost of production and, in the case of military hardware, would be included in the price paid for such goods by the Ministry of Defense. However, a 1960 decree established a new Machinery Development Fund which spreads the cost of developing new machinery (in the machine building and metalworking industries) over all producing enterprises. Thus developmental costs would not be fully reflected in prices of goods in those sectors of industry where new products play a particularly important role, as compared with sectors producing more traditional types of output.

Obviously, the defense industry is a primary example of a sector where technology is rapidly changing. In such an industry, development of new items may be a significant portion of total costs. Not very much is known about the pricing of military goods; however, a great deal of information is available on the financing of developmental costs in general in Soviet industry. Prior to the 1960 decree, such costs (including preparation of experimental models, and adapting machinery and factory space to the new production) were charged to the cost of production of the new model being developed, and were distributed over the cost of output for the initial two years of production. This procedure was criticized as being the cause for excessively high prices for new products. Also, even after the second year of production, when the developmental costs had already been recouped, the initial high prices were often retained, resulting in excessively high profits for the producing enterprises. Beginning in January 1961, however, all planned outlays for the creation of new models in the machine building and metalworking industries have been charged to a special fund created from sums charged to the cost of production of all enterprises in these industries. Prices for the new products are set comparable to prices of earlier developed similar products, taking into account the technical or economic advantage of the new product for the user. Thus the cost of developing a new product is covered not from the production of that particular product, but from the production of all products in that branch. Since the defense industry must use a proportionally larger share of funds for developing new products than nondefense machinery and metalworking industries, this is another example of possible subsidization of the defense industry by other industry. In 1965, the Machinery Development Fund was expanded to include several additional branches of the economy. Soviet sources make it clear that these charges to the cost of production are limited to civilian output (Gallik et al., 1968, p. 147). However, they may still be used as an indirect subsidy for assimilating costs of defense products (Nolting, 1973, p. 30).

Developmental outlays for weapons can be financed in various other ways. Sums for this purpose come from the science allocation, under Social-Cultural Measures (see the Appendix), but they probably pertain to the earlier research stages. In addition, the budget makes grants for developmental outlays under the Financing the National Economy category, though there is no way of estimating the amount. Finally, enterprise profit may be used for research outlays, but here the sums are known to be small.

## F. Nonbudget Funds (Vnebiudzhetnye Sredstva)

These funds, which by their nature do not appear to be of much significance, are often mentioned in the literature and are therefore listed here as another part of the aggregate financial balance. They consist of the special income of organizations and institutions which are financed entirely by the budget. Even though they are financed by the budget, some of the income of these organizations is not deposited into the budget but is deposited in a special account in the Gosbank and used for specific purposes. Some sources of *vnebiudzhetnye sredstva* are: income from the productive activity of subsidiary enterprises; income from buildings belonging to budget organizations (rent); payment for services of budget institutions (e.g., for looking over plans and accounts in construction); income from laboratory and scientific work; some school payments, museum fees, etc.; and deductions of economic organizations for preparing cadres (Plotnikov, 1959, pp. 379-380; Aleksandrov, 1961, pp. 418-420).

One can conceive how some of these funds might be used for military purposes. Suppose the Ministry of Defense receives subsidiary income from selling surplus stocks. It could use these funds for military purposes.[e] There is evidence that some scientific research is supported by such funds. Scientific research institutes and

---

[e]Apparently the Ministry of Defense does sell some goods, because we know its sales (except for those of military publications) are exempt from turnover tax (Kovylin, 1963, p. 95). Also the Ministry of Defense does have some type of subordinate industrial enterprises (Allakhverdian, 1962, p. 310).

higher educational establishments perform work on contract for state enterprises and economic organizations. But in general, this appears to be on a very small scale (in 1959 the amount of work planned to be done on contract by higher educational establishments was 45 million rubles) and not necessarily of a military nature. More generally, these funds, in accordance with their sources as indicated earlier, are spent for the repair of buildings, support of museums, travel expenses of individuals finishing higher education, and the like.

## G. Foreign Trade

Apparently imports and exports of military equipment are not included explicitly in the Soviet foreign trade statistical handbooks. The handbooks do say that commodities of a "noncommercial" character are excluded and this may be the rubric under which materiel is classified. On the other hand, there is some evidence to suggest that while military commodities are not itemized in the trade handbooks, they are included in the totals. This is adduced from the fact that the discrepancy between the total exports and the sums of itemized items accords, roughly, with independent estimates of drawings on Soviet military credits (see also Kostinsky, 1974).

Whichever the case, the fact that military goods are not easily identifiable has led some observers to argue that a military buildup might be disguised by exporting nonmilitary goods and using the foreign exchange proceeds to import military goods. This problem does not appear to be a real one. A military good that might be imported is originally paid for by the foreign trade combine which manages the transaction. The combine does not keep it, however. It sells the item to the Ministry of Defense, to the State Reserve agency, or what have you. At this point, the item is recorded as an expenditure, the procedure being identical with that which would have occurred if production had been domestic.

The only problem is in the sphere of verification. If imports of military goods exceed exports, domestic expenditures for procurement of hardware will exceed output; if exports exceed imports, output will exceed expenditures for procurement.

# 5 Verification by Financial Means

## A. Problem of Definitions

It is not at all impossible that a considerable part of the verification problem, as it appears to investigators at the moment, might be eliminated by a mutually agreed-upon definition of terms. Both nations fail to include in the military appropriations items which could be defined as military expenditures. In the absence of a definition of military expenditures, it is quite natural that differences exist and that there are ambiguities regarding the respective military efforts of the two nations. Certainly a first and necessary step in any such conference on arms control should be an attempt to agree upon the definition and scope of "military expenditures." It may turn out, for example, that if it is agreed that military R&D or veterans' pensions are defined as part of defense expenditure, the Soviets will agree to make these expenditures explicit in their accounts or agree to include them under "defense" if not already there. It is also possible, of course, that even after such an agreement they may resort to further subterfuge. But certainly, nothing is lost, and something may be gained by a definition of terms. Definition of terms does not, however, eliminate the problem of verification; it merely simplifies it.

Let us now assume that "military expenditure" has been defined. Then, assuming different possible loci of clandestine expenditure, what are the corresponding steps in the process of verification?

## B. The Budget Expenditures

As we have suggested, most Western experts feel that if there are undisclosed military expenditures, they are hidden somewhere in the budget. As a reasonable first step, then, and one which could not lightly be refused by a nation pretending to serious consideration of arms control and reduction, the Soviet government should be asked to present its budget expenditures fully (i.e., eliminating residuals of sizable dimensions) and in greater detail. More detail would be wanted for both defense and nondefense categories: in the latter case, so that it can more easily be determined what military expenditures might be left out of explicit defense; in the former case, to facilitate verification operations. In either case, one would hope that the extensive detail presented by the U.S. Budget might serve as inspiration, although such extensive detail would never be provided and certainly is not necessary to verification.[a]

How can one be sure that the figures, as presented, are correct? Several requirements might be imposed which would enhance the reliability of the information.

First, it might be required that the additional data be published by the USSR as part of its regular annual budget. If the data are legitimate, there should be no excuse for not publishing them. To the extent that the data were not published for security reasons, this obstacle presumably is removed when the data are handed to the major antagonist, the United States. Publication should be required because, in my opinion, the Soviets would have at least as great, perhaps even greater, inhibitions about publishing falsified data than they would about handing these data over to a disarmament commission or to the United States. This statement is based partly on the fact that, in the opinion of most Western scholars, there have been very few instances (if any) over the past 55 years of publication by the Soviets of deliberately falsified data, despite many examples of "withholding," "misleading," and so forth. The publication of falsified data would, it should be noted, serve an extremely dysfunctional role internally, since published data do serve as a basis for the work done by most Soviet scholars not directly connected with central planning as well as many engaged in planning.[b] This, in fact, is certainly one of the reasons they have preferred, in the past, to withhold rather than to falsify.

Second, it might be required that the budget accounts for the past, say, 5 or 10 years be published in the same detail and form as is

---

[a]In this chapter we do not consider the problems relating to the kinds of information we would have to give the Soviets in exchange for the information requested by us and the net advantage or disadvantage of the total exchange.

[b]While the greater security controls exercised within the Soviet government might make it less necessary to classify materials within the government, in fact their greater preoccupation with security undoubtedly results in allowing very few persons to have access to confidential data of the sort we are concerned with.

to be required in the future (this general approach is suggested by Morris Bornstein, 1963). This would create very substantial constraints to the future manipulation and falsification, for two reasons. First, the budgetary data already published provide a rigid framework within which the new detailed data must fit. (This, of course, presents an obstacle to falsification even if additional historical data are not made available.) Second, the detailed historical data then provide a trend framework into which present and future details must fit. Over and above these constraints on falsification, the historical data would have the additional virtue of possibly resolving many of the uncertainties and questions Western scholars have had in the past regarding Soviet defense expenditures. This in itself would give us a better "feel" for Soviet budget data and more confidence and know-how for evaluating future data. Third, the historical data enable us to perform significance tests, to be described presently.

Assume that the Soviets have given us substantial additional budgetary expenditure information as suggested above. How would we go about verifying claimed reductions in defense expenditures and how large would a reduction have to be to be identifiable? These questions are basically the kinds of questions that should be answered by a competent statistician, which I am not. What follows, therefore, should be considered primarily suggestive.

The basic hypothesis of this section, to repeat, is that defense expenditures may be hidden in other budget expenditure accounts. If this is the case, then these other accounts should show significant deviations from their past trends (trends having been fitted). How would one decide what is a "significant deviation" from past trends? The usual rule of thumb in these matters is to consider as highly unlikely to be due to chance, any point which deviates from trend in one direction (in this case, upward) by as much as, or more than, 1.645 standard deviations.[c] Therefore, all other things being equal, a reduction in military expenditures which is large enough to be identifiable is one that would cause deviations from trend in other budget expenditures of 1.645 standard deviations. This means, of course, that "identifiability" as defined here depends not only on the size of the reduction in military expenditures, but also on the degree to

[c]More precisely, one can be 95 percent confident that any point which is 1.645 standard deviations above trend deviates for nonrandom reasons. The U.S., in these circumstances, may wish to observe more conservative standards, regarding suspiciously smaller deviations from trend (smaller probabilities of clandestine expenditures).

which individual budget expenditures tend to fluctuate around their trends. Thus a 15 percent reduction in military expenditures may be identifiable if the standard deviations from trends of other items are small, but unidentifiable if large. Furthermore, the more detailed the budget expenditure data provided by the Soviets, the more likely it would be that a given amount of clandestine expenditures would cause significant deviations in individual items.[d]

There are serious difficulties with the application of this technique to detecting clandestine expenditures. First, the analysis is based on the assumption that the trends in other budget expenditures have been generated more or less randomly, an assumption which may well not be true and which would, in any event, be difficult to check.

Second, identifiability will depend to some extent on how clandestine expenditures are hidden. If, for example, they are hidden in 10 percent (by value) of other expenditure items, the deviations from trends might well be relatively large; if, on the other hand, they are spread evenly throughout the whole budget, the deviations from trends of individual items might be small, indeed, with little possibility of identification in the sense already defined. Fortunately, for purposes of verification, it would seem most probable that if military expenditures are hidden among other expenditure items, these would be limited in number because of the very great inconvenience of spreading them widely. In fact, faced with the necessity of spreading clandestine expenditures widely over the whole budget, it would seem in order for a nation to consider seriously setting up separate secret accounts as a simpler alternative (see description in Chapter 5, Section D).

Third, and this may be the most serious stumbling block to verification, there may not be means of distinguishing the hiding of clandestine expenditures in "other" budget expenditure categories from the normal (in the Soviet case) adjustment of the budget to real compliance with the terms of an arms reduction agreement. If the Soviets truly reduced defense expenditures by, say, 15 percent, they would immediately plan to use the released resources elsewhere. If these resources were used for increasing investment, research, education, health, foreign aid, or any other activities financed through

---

[d]A useful experiment would be to establish trends and calculate standard deviations for items in the U.S. and Soviet budgets for, say, 1940-1970, and then see how well 1971-1974 can be predicted. See the estimate made at the end of Chapter 5, Section D.

the budget, these items would correspondingly increase dispropor-tionately (to trend) just as though they were repositories of clandes-tine military expenditures. To the extent, of course, that factories which produced tanks were converted (for example) to tractors (purchased by the collective farms) or resources were diverted to consumption, other budget expenditures would not rise by a corres-ponding amount and identification would still be possible. Identifi-cation would also be possible if there were an increase in other budget expenditure categories which were totally unrelated to de-fense in a resource substitution sense (such as civilian pensions). However, it seems highly probable that a large percentage of the released resources would, in fact, be purchased through the budget under some other, relevant heading. This weakens the possibility of unambiguously identifying clandestine expenditures[e] and would put the United States in the position of running the risk of sounding frequent false alarms.[f]

The only way of getting around this particular problem, it seems to me, is for the United States to have some rights of audit, where particular Soviet expenditure items deviate suspiciously from trend, to determine whether the deviation is due to the inclusion of clandes-tine items or to proper increases. The audit need not constitute a substantial intrusion on Soviet privacy. A very small random sample of expenditure vouchers would enable one to tell with a high degree of probability and confidence whether or not the increase was due to clandestine military expenditures. Since sampling problems and techniques are discussed in Chapter 6, Section A, they will not be elaborated here.

We have stressed, so far, the use of the budget expenditure data to track down clandestine expenditures within the budget itself, without examining other financial accounts or other economic data.

[e]A similar problem exists in connection with the use of input-output type methods for verification. If a nation reduces the number of tanks it is producing but immediately increases the number of tractors by the same amount, one cannot verify the armament reduction by checking steel production or production of other inputs used in the production of both commodities.

[f]Verification of arms reduction by the United States would be easier for two reasons. First, not having as active a full-employment policy as the Soviets, reductions in U.S. military expendi-tures would not be compensated for elsewhere in the economy as rapidly. Furthermore, monetary as well as fiscal policy would be used by the United States so that our budget would probably reflect less of the compensatory activity than would be the case in the USSR. Second, since military expenditures are a considerably larger part of the U.S. budget than of the Soviet budget, reductions in military expenditures are more detectable in the budget accounts themselves.

The provision of additional budgetary data may also make it possible to detect clandestine expenditures by comparison of these data with the large amounts of nonbudget data which have been made available in recent years. The technique of detection is essentially the same as that just described for budgetary expenditure data per se. Suppose, for example, the Soviets give us a breakdown of their defense appropriation for each year of the postwar period including, say, the payroll of the armed forces. Suppose we also have a series for the civilian payroll for the same period. If there is an arms reduction agreement and the military payroll declines, then we would expect the civilian payroll to rise relative to trend, perhaps with a lag, because of the conversion of soldiers to civilian life or the decline in the number of new draftees. If the civilian payroll did not rise relative to trend, then one would suspect that the Soviet figures were untruthful. As before, a 95 percent confidence level would be achieved if the civilian payroll figure deviated from trend by 1.645 standard deviations.

Whether or not this particular test is any good would depend on the extent of fluctuations around the civilian payroll trend and the size of the military payroll (relative to the civilian payroll) in the first place. It could be, for example, that the total military payroll was less than 1.645 standard deviations, in which case the test would be powerless. This points up a very important though obvious principle, namely that it is essential to find and use relationships in which nondefense activities are sensitive to changes in defense expenditures. This principle should be a guideline in determining the kinds of breakdowns of defense and nondefense budgetary material we want from the Russians.

We leave budget expenditures for the moment. More general methods of verification will be described in Chapter 6. We also consider the pricing problem separately (Chapter 5, Section G), since it applies to military expenditures whereever they may be located.

## C. The Budget Surplus: Hidden Budget Expenditures

It was suggested earlier that the Soviets conceivably might not report at all some budgeted military expenditures, with the result that the reported budget surplus would be spuriously large. This possibility is not considered as likely as those previously mentioned. Moreover, it seems probable that if expenditures are not reported, a like amount of receipts would also remain unreported, leaving the surplus unchanged—a possibility considered in Section D of this chapter. Nevertheless, because of ambiguities in connection with the Soviet budget surplus considered earlier, it is worth considering how to check on hidden expenditures.

Since a combination of unreported expenditures and fully reported receipts leads to a spuriously large budget surplus, the most obvious method of verification is to check on the disposition of the budget surplus. As noted earlier, the budget surplus is supposed, with some minor exceptions, to be deposited in the budget's account in the Gosbank. While the Soviets do not publish consistent data on this account, they have published enough sporadic information to suggest that they do not consider it "secret." As a first step, an attempt should be made to obtain this figure or have it made available as part of the budgetary picture (along with any other disposition made of the surplus along lines suggested earlier). If the figure is obtained from the existing literature, it may provide a good check. On the other hand, if requested from the Russians, it simply pushes the problem of verification back one step further, since it obviously can be falsified.

The next step in verification would be to ask that the entire balance sheet of the Gosbank be made available. This request may be hard to justify. As one gets further and further away from the ostensible sources of military expenditures, namely the budget, one will have a harder and harder time justifying demands for additional data. In this request, one would face resistance due to the fact that the Soviets apparently regard certain items in the balance sheet as sacrosanct, especially "gold and foreign exchange" and "cash (notes) in circulation."

If the balance sheets are provided, the question then becomes: Are the figures truthful? The verification problem here is similar to that posed by budget expenditures. Since some figures are available from the recent past, these provide constraints on the ways in which the present figures might be falsified. However, our information on recent Gosbank balance sheets is sufficiently scattered that quite a few degrees of freedom for misrepresentation exist. On the other hand, there are some relationships that might be checked: for example, the relation between cash in circulation and both personal money income (which can be estimated fairly accurately) and retail trade turnover (adjusted for savings).[g] If the Soviets could be prevailed upon to publish not only current Gosbank figures but also those from the recent past, checks such as the above would be much more reliable; in addition, a series of trends would be available which would provide additional constraints against falsification.

Some of the same problems of identification which confronted us in connection with budget expenditures in the previous section confront us here. The procedure here would parallel that followed above. Identification would probably be easier, for two reasons. First, the clandestine expenditures would probably loom larger in relation to changes in Gosbank accounts than they would in relation to budget accounts. Second, it is unlikely, in the event of true compliance with an arms reduction agreement, that short-term credit extended by the Gosbank would correspondingly increase (as was the case with the budget). On the other hand, casual empiricism leads us to believe that the standard deviations from trends of items in the Gosbank accounts tend to be larger than those in the budget accounts, thereby making identification more difficult.

## D. Separate Secret Accounts

Removal from the budget of an equal amount of receipts and expenditures in order to avoid disclosure of certain military expenditures would seem to be a possibility if nonconformity with an arms control agreement were desired. While there are almost no functional relationships on the expenditure side which would aid in the detection of such clandestine items, "some" possibility of verification exists with regard to receipts, although not with the data currently available.

The possibilities are highlighted by the quite successful calculation by Abram Bergson (1953, Appendix E) of turnover tax receipts for 1937. The turnover tax receipts for 1937 were reported by the Soviets as amounting to 7.59 billion rubles. In his 1937 book Bergson calculated, from diverse indirect evidence, that 1.59 billion rubles were collected from miscellaneous nonconsumer goods sources such as communal services, inventories, government administra-

---

[g]It is also worth noting that any attempt to hide military expenditures in the Gosbank accounts would require falsification by the Soviets of both assets and liabilities.

tion, etc. This left 6 billion rubles to be accounted for as a residual by sales of consumers' goods. A reestimate (Bergson, 1961, Appendix I) in 1961 resulted in a residual of 6.19 billion rubles. Then Bergson, with the help of Herbert Levine, made a direct calculation of turnover tax receipts "by commodity" based on commodity figures provided by Janet Chapman (1963) and turnover tax rates published in the Soviet handbooks. The direct calculation yielded a figure of 6.048 billion rubles, a fairly close approximation. For present purposes, unfortunately, turnover tax rates have not been systematically published since World War II.

Other similar estimations are possible on the receipts side. The social insurance markup (or payroll tax) can be estimated from legislation regarding its rates and the aggregate wage bill. Very close approximations along these lines have been made. It is also possible to make estimates of the income tax from the legislation regarding its schedules and scattered information regarding personal income and its distribution. Several other small items may also be estimated with varying degrees of confidence.

The difficulties with attempting to check on the existence of separate accounts by reconstructing receipts are that, with the information now available or available in the past, (a) the range of error on estimable items is in the aggregate large, and unless the separate accounts are very large they would be hard to detect with any degree of certitude; (b) the deductions from profits, a very large receipts item, is basically a residual item and does not have a rate structure which would permit estimation as in the case of the turnover tax; (c) there are a number of unspecified small items among receipts on which not much information has ever been published; and (d) the Soviets have a propensity to engage, on occasion, in unconventional budgetary accounting, as noted above.

If it happened that separate accounts were implemented by reducing, say, just the receipts from the turnover tax, identification might be possible. This would seem to be the simplest device, administratively. On the other hand, if the hidden receipts were spread over many revenue categories, identification would be very difficult. Much of the discussion of identification in Chapter 6 (Section A) would be applicable here.

If separate accounts are considered a serious possibility, then the arms control agreement should require the Soviets to publish the revenue side of their budget in greater detail so that all sources of receipts are itemized. As with expenditures, the provision of historical data in the same detail for the development of trends would also be useful for verification. Given these data, as many functional relationships as possible should be established for future estimation purposes. Many of these relationships will be impossible to establish in the absence of availability of the laws and changes in the laws on such things as turnover tax rates. This type of information should be part of the package.

From the preceding discussion, it should be clear that the identification of secret budgetary accounts would be difficult indeed by the methods suggested so far if the Soviets made serious attempts to hide such accounts. On the other hand, if they are willing to provide all the data suggested earlier, which seems unlikely, then it may well be difficult for them to hide accounts successfully, although it probably could be done.

Finally, it should be noted that if separate secret accounts were established, the total budget would be reduced by the amount of these accounts. (We assume that if military expenditures are really reduced, the Soviet government would immediately spend the freed funds, through the budget, on nonmilitary activities. Actually, there might be some lag in this process, and all funds might not be respent, thus reducing the significance of our test.) Would the removal of these accounts be identifiable? The same standard can be applied here as was suggested for individual budget expenditures in Section B of this chapter: establish the growth trend of the budget and regard suspiciously any deviations from this trend which exceed 1.645 standard deviations (required for one-tail test with 95 percent level of confidence). For illustrative purposes, the linear trend for Soviet budget expenditures was computed on the basis of unadjusted figures for the years 1962-1973. The regression equation is

$$Y = 52.56 + 9.72\,X,$$

where $Y$ is the estimated budget expenditure figure and $X$ represents time. The standard deviation from trend is 4.533 billion rubles, and 1.645 standard deviations from trend is 7.96 billion rubles.

Suppose we were trying to decide whether the Soviets had established separate secret accounts in 1974 to hide military expenditures to avoid compliance with an arms reduction agreement! How large would the reduction (and the clandestine accounts) have to be to be identifiable at the 95 percent confidence level? Basically, the reduction would have to be about 7.46 billion rubles, or 1.645 standard deviations. Since announced defense expenditures amounted to 17.9 billion rubles in 1973, this means that the agreed-upon arms reduction would have to have been extremely large to be identifiable—a reduction of 41 percent,[h] all of which is removed from the budget. This particular calculation is clearly not a very powerful test for separate secret accounts in the Soviet case. More powerful tests can probably be devised, however, by using more sophisticated statistical techniques.

A further method of check is suggested in Chapter 6.

## E.  Bank Credit

As we have already suggested, it seems unlikely that military expenditures would be channeled through the banking system in the guise of extensions of credit. The method of check on this possibility is roughly similar to that used for budget expenditures: to request from the Russians as detailed an account as possible of the distribution of the annual increment to loans outstanding, along with as many historical data as they can be prevailed upon to provide. The ways in which this might inhibit falsification were discussed previously in connection with budget expenditures.

## F.  Retained Profits, Amortization Funds, and Other "Sources" of Expenditures

Retained profits of enterprises are the only serious "source" of other expenditures which might be used for clandestine purposes. We therefore neglect the others, though the method of verification is similar, since all these funds appear to have the same repositories —the Gosbank and the Stroibank.

In functional terms, the retained profits of state enterprises and their distribution are preponderantly a substitute for deductions

---

[h]To the budget expenditures of 1973 of 184.3 billion rubles, we would add the trend of 9.72 for a total predicted budget of 194.02 in 1974. If the 1974 budget then totaled only 186.56 billion rubles (194.02 − 7.456), we could be 95 percent confident that the Soviets had set up separate secret accounts. In the earlier version of this study, completed in 1965, we ran a regression based on budget expenditures for 1945-1962. In this case the fit was better, and it would have been possible to detect a 30 percent reduction in military expenditures at the 95 percent confidence level.

from profits to the budget and expenditures on Financing the National Economy which, for administrative reasons, have been slightly decentralized. While it is true that these particular receipts presumably could not be directed easily to purchases for defense, they are in practice as suspect as any other nondefense category in the budget. Therefore, it is certainly appropriate to ask the Russians for a detailed accounting (present and past, if possible) of such expenditures at the same time that the request is made for more detail on budget expenditures as a whole.

Verification on the basis of these additional data, however, would be somewhat more difficult than verification of regular budgetary expenditures, because of the smaller amount of information that has been available on them in the past. Thus, with respect to profits, the Soviets would not be as constrained to present accurate information as with budget expenditures; they would have more freedom to manipulate the accounts.

Verification would also be more difficult because of the fact that some profits are netted (as outlined above), and this provides wide scope for falsification and for the diversion of funds to clandestine military uses. There would be constraints on these possibilities if there were information on the degree of grossness or netness of profits in the past. To our knowledge, there is none.[1] In fact, since much of the netting of profits is accomplished autonomously by enterprises and ministries, and since the amounts involved are not particularly relevant from an overall financial point of view, it is possible that the Soviet authorities themselves do not know the precise extent of the practice.

If the gross-net distortions are not serious, other checks, aside from evaluating trends based on detailed accounts, are possible. For example, the bulk of nonagricultural investment in the economy is made either via the budget or out of retained profits of enterprises. Comparison of budgeted investment plus retained profits with total nonagricultural (including investment in state farms, excluding investment by collective farms) investment might be suggestive. However, such a check would probably not be precise enough for arms control purposes.

So far, we have not been able to suggest any very reliable methods of verifying that retained profits of enterprises are not spent

---

[1]This does not imply that profits were netted in the past and that the degree of netness was hidden in order to deceive. Undoubtedly these practices were "benign."

for military purposes. (Further techniques are suggested in Chapter 6.) However, it seems doubtful that profits have been used either deliberately or extensively in the past for such purposes. Nevertheless, they remain a potential loophole in the event of an arms control agreement.

## G. Pricing Problems

The pricing problems outlined earlier affect verification of military expenditures regardless of source. Two aspects of the problem were noted. First is the fact that the real costs and monetary costs at the time of an agreement may diverge because of differential subsidies and sales taxes. Second, the extent of disarmament can be obscured by changes in prices effected by carefully maneuvered changes in subsidies and sales taxes.

It is very difficult to envision a solution to the first problem, especially when one views the probable counter-requests by the Soviets for figures on such things as the relative percentage of (private enterprise) profits in the various commodities purchased by the U.S. government for defense purposes. Despite this difficulty from the American point of view, agreement should be obtained, at least in principle, with the proposition that the initial reduction is not to include turnover taxes on consumers' goods (if military procurements do include such taxes?). Correspondingly, of course, it would be appropriate for the Soviets to add to their claimed reduction in expenditures, subsidies on commodities which are being eliminated. This problem is serious from our point of view only if the Soviets have (a) a considerable amount of turnover tax on items which are low in priority and would be the first to go in an arms control agreement, (b) large subsidies to the highest-priority material which would not be reduced in a general expenditure reduction agreement. In fact, if the RAND estimates for 1956-1958 by Nancy Nimitz (1962, pp. 141, 146) are accurate, subsidies and sales taxes, while not inconsequential, are nevertheless not likely to be sources of major error. For 1958, turnover taxes are estimated to have constituted roughly 6 percent of total military outlays, or .58 billion rubles out of a total of 9.06 billion rubles. The "average effective rate" of 25 percent is assumed by Nimitz to apply to military subsistence purchased by the Defense Ministry. If there were a 15 percent reduction in military expenditures (in 1958) and subsistence were reduced by as much as 30 percent,[j] or a total reduction of 1.36 billion rubles, turnover tax would amount to only .11 billion rubles. That is, if Nimitz's assumptions are correct, the arms reduction would be 14 percent in real terms instead of the nominal 15 percent.

Subsidies on military goods would appear to be even less of a problem statistically than turnover taxes, amounting in 1958 to only .2 billion rubles by RAND estimates. If this figure is at all close to the real order of magnitude of subsidies to the military, then the degree of possible manipulation as calculated in the preceding paragraph could not be substantially altered.

The more serious problem would seem to me to be the second one, that further reductions in military expenditures over time could be effected by simply reducing prices, either by reducing turnover taxes or by increasing subsidies. The greater scope for deception over time exists in connection with the subsidies, which in theory can be increased indefinitely, whereas turnover taxes can only be reduced to zero from present levels, which, by RAND estimates, are not very large. One possible solution to this problem would be for the Soviets to agree, along lines discussed previously in connection with budget expenditures, to present their budget expenditure accounts in greater detail. Any substantial change in subsidies would certainly be suspect. Of course, if the actual items to which subsidies were applied were truthfully listed, there would be no problem at all.

A more direct approach to the problem would be to include in the disarmament agreement a provision which specified that agreed-upon reductions in expenditures shall be in "real" terms. For purposes of implementation, each nation would be required to provide a price index of its military expenditures. If the details of the index were not specified, there would be room for manipulation and evasion. (Even if they were specified, of course, the index could still be faked.) Items which were planned to be subsidized in order to feign a reduction in expenditures could be assigned a very small weight or left out of the index entirely to hide clues concerning the existence of newly granted subsidies.[k] If the Soviets have determined to cheat in the manner indicated, there does not appear to be any simple way of

---

[j]Presumably there are constraints on how much one can manipulate the proportions of the reduction mix. This estimate takes no account of subsidies.

[k]If the prices of items purchased by the military were presented in detail, detection could still be avoided by presenting cost-prices, that is, prices before subsidies.

checking on the validity of the index in the absence of full-scale information on the index and access to the accounts for verification purposes. However, given reasonably detailed information on budget expenditures of the sort envisaged earlier, large-scale subsidization may be detectable elsewhere in the budget where the subsidy is recorded.

It is also possible that prices may rise or fall as a result of actual legitimate changes in costs of production. In this event, it would be in the Soviet interests, if they did not want to reduce military expenditures, to disguise the fact that prices had fallen (if they had). This would enable them to then reduce the nominal value of their military expenditures without a comparable reduction in real value. This seems less likely to happen because (1) producers' goods prices are not changed very frequently and (2) price handbooks exist and general movements in prices can be approximated by Western scholars. However, it is possible that with the relatively stable factor-cost structure the Soviets have experienced since 1948, many items of military production might experience sharp reductions in costs as new methods were introduced and large-scale production was achieved. This is particularly true in military production because of the rapid pace of technical change and the speed of introduction of new techniques. While this certainly could be a source of evasion, it is hard to believe that it could happen on a sufficient scale over short periods of time to be significant.

## H. The Financial Balance

The USSR Central Statistical Administration (TsSU) has been compiling a detailed balance of the national economy since 1957. This balance, consisting of 7 tables and 11 appendixes, is not made public, although the general form has been presented and published. The two balances that would seem most relevant to verification are the so-called Materials Balance, or "Balance of Production, Consumption, and Accumulation of Social Product," and the Financial Balance, or "Balance of Production, Distribution, and Redistribution of the Social Product and National Income in the National Economy." Either of these two balances would be useful for verification purposes if they were available in greater detail. As they are presented, they both suffer from the main defect of the budget itself, namely that military items are lumped together with other items. So, for example, in the Materials Balance, investment in military facilities is probably included in "Growth of basic funds" in column 13, military procurement probably included with "administration" in column 11, and so forth (see Table 5-1). Without great detail, the Materials Balance by itself would be much less revealing than the budget and practically useless for purposes of financial verification.

The basic Financial Balance is somewhat more detailed than the Materials Balance and is somewhat more useful to us because the categories in which it is presented are financial and can be related more easily to the budget and to the banking system. The basic advantage of the Financial Balance (also the Materials Balance) over the budget is the fact that it is not a two-way balance like the budget (which need not balance), but rather a matrix in which a large number of financial interrelationships are specified. Moreover, it includes nonbudget as well as budget and bank financial flows.

The basic categories of the Financial Balance are presented in Table 5-2. Columns 1-9 list the production and primary distribution of social product and national income. Here, receipts from sales of material production (column 1) are classified first as "Value of means of production transferred to the product" (column 2) and second as total national income (column 8); the latter is subdivided into payments to the population (columns 3-6) and the "Fund for the satisfaction of social needs" (column 7) financed largely by the turnover tax and profits; net transfer of primary income is listed in column 9.

Columns 11-37 trace transfer of primary income generated in the productive sphere through the economy. Columns 11-22 list transfer items including payments to the budget and banking system (columns 11-16), outlays for services (column 17), wages paid to workers in nonproductive spheres such as health and education (column 18), enterprise direct outlays for nonproductive ends (on-the-job training, housing, etc.; column 19), direct support of the population (in rest homes, armed forces, etc.; column 20), growth of money in circulation (column 21), and increases in credit balances (column 22).

Columns 23-37 list the distribution of the transferred sums in the form of receipts from the budget and the financial system, from sale of services, from direct outlays of enterprises for nonproductive

## Table 5-1
## Balance of Production, Consumption, and Accumulation of Social Product (Materials Balance)

|  | Production | | | | | | | Distribution | | | | | | | | | |
|  | | | | | | | | Consumption | | | | | Accumulation | | | | |
|  | (1) | (2) | (3) | (4) | (5) | (6) | (7) | (8) | (9) | (10) | (11) | (12) | (13) | (14) | (15) | (16) | (17) |
|  | Produced during the year in producers' prices (by social form) | Addition to value in sphere of distribution (by social form) of which: | In transport (by social form) | In trade, procurement, material supply (by social form) | Sent abroad | Total output in consumers' prices | Productive material outlays (by branch and social form) | Private consumption of population (by social form) | In cultural, welfare institutions | In scientific institutions | In administration | Total consumption by society | Growth of basic funds (by branch and social form) | Growth of material working funds and reserves (by branch and social form) | Growth of reserves / Total | Losses (by branch and social form) | Sent abroad |
|---|---|---|---|---|---|---|---|---|---|---|---|---|---|---|---|---|---|
| Means of production |  |  |  |  |  |  |  |  |  |  |  |  |  |  |  |  |  |
| Industrial products |  |  |  |  |  |  |  |  |  |  |  |  |  |  |  |  |  |
| Agricultural products |  |  |  |  |  |  |  |  |  |  |  |  |  |  |  |  |  |
| Forestry products |  |  |  |  |  |  |  |  |  |  |  |  |  |  |  |  |  |
| Construction products |  |  |  |  |  |  |  |  |  |  |  |  |  |  |  |  |  |
| Communication production |  |  |  |  |  |  |  |  |  |  |  |  |  |  |  |  |  |
| Objects for consumption |  |  |  |  |  |  |  |  |  |  |  |  |  |  |  |  |  |
| Industrial products |  |  |  |  |  |  |  |  |  |  |  |  |  |  |  |  |  |
| Agricultural products |  |  |  |  |  |  |  |  |  |  |  |  |  |  |  |  |  |
| Construction products |  |  |  |  |  |  |  |  |  |  |  |  |  |  |  |  |  |
| Products for public dining |  |  |  |  |  |  |  |  |  |  |  |  |  |  |  |  |  |
| Total national economy |  |  |  |  |  |  |  |  |  |  |  |  |  |  |  |  |  |
| Industrial products |  |  |  |  |  |  |  |  |  |  |  |  |  |  |  |  |  |
| Agricultural products |  |  |  |  |  |  |  |  |  |  |  |  |  |  |  |  |  |
| Forestry products |  |  |  |  |  |  |  |  |  |  |  |  |  |  |  |  |  |
| Construction products |  |  |  |  |  |  |  |  |  |  |  |  |  |  |  |  |  |
| Products for public dining |  |  |  |  |  |  |  |  |  |  |  |  |  |  |  |  |  |
| Communication production |  |  |  |  |  |  |  |  |  |  |  |  |  |  |  |  |  |

Source: V. A. Sobol', *Ocherki po voprosam balansa narodnogo khoziaistva*, Moscow 1960, Table 3.

# Table 5-2
# Balance of Production, Distribution, and Redistribution of the Social Product and National Income in the National Economy (Financial Balance) (millions of rubles)

| | Production and Primary Distribution of the Social Product and National Income | | | | | | | | | Redistribution of the Social Product and National Income — Paid Out | | | | | | | | | | | | |
| | Social product produced | Value of means of production transferred to the product | Wages and salaries | Income on collective farms (payment for work units) | Other earned income | Total | Fund for the satisfaction of social needs (the commodity as a social category) | Total national income | Primary incomes, paid out (−), received (+) | Received from outside sources | Total contributed by enterprises, establishments, and the population by way of redistribution | To the State Budget | To the State insurance system | To the social insurance system | To the credit system | To the savings banks | Payment for services | Wages and salaries paid by nonproductive organizations | Direct contributions by enterprises of productive branches for the maintenance of nonproductive branches | Material benefits supplied to the population by nonproductive organizations | Increase in cash in hand | Increase of debtor liabilities |
|---|---|---|---|---|---|---|---|---|---|---|---|---|---|---|---|---|---|---|---|---|---|---|
| | 1 | 2 | 3 | 4 | 5 | 6 | 7 | 8 | 9 | 10 | 11 | 12 | 13 | 14 | 15 | 16 | 17 | 18 | 19 | 20 | 21 | 22 |
| **A. Enterprises of branches engaged in material production** | | | | | | | | | | | | | | | | | | | | | | |
| **I. By social forms** | | | | | | | | | | | | | | | | | | | | | | |
| a) State | | | | | | | | | | x | | | | | | | | x | | x | | |
| b) Cooperative and collective farm | | | | | | | | | | x | | | | | | | | x | | x | | |
| of which collective farm | | | | | | | | | | x | | | | | | | | x | | x | | |
| c) Subsidiary economies of collective farmers | | | x | x | | | x | | | x | | | | x | | x | | x | x | x | | x |
| d) Subsidiary economies of workers and employees | | | x | x | | | x | | | x | | | | x | | x | | x | x | x | | x |
| Total | | | | | | | | | | x | | | | | | | | x | | x | | |
| **II. By branches** | | | | | | | | | | | | | | | | | | | | | | |
| 1. Industry | | | | | | | | | | x | | | | | | | | x | | x | | |
| 2. Agriculture | | | | | | | | | | x | | | | | | | | x | | x | | |
| 3. Forestry | | | | | | | | | | x | | | | | | | | x | | x | | |
| 4. Building and construction | | | | | | | | | | x | | | | | | | | x | | x | | |
| 5. Transport and communications | | | | | | | | | | x | | | | | | | | x | | x | | |
| 6. Trade, procurement, material and technical supplies | | | | | | | | | | x | | | | | | | | x | | x | | |

## Table 5-2 (continued)

| | Redistribution of the Social Product and National Income | | | | | | | | | | | | | | | Final utilization of Social Product and National Income for the Year | | | | | |
| --- | --- | --- | --- | --- | --- | --- | --- | --- | --- | --- | --- | --- | --- | --- | --- | --- | --- | --- | --- | --- | --- |
| | Received | | | | | | | | | | | | | | | | including | | | | |
| | | of which | | | | | | | | | | | | | | | | | Accumulation | | |
| Total received by enterprises, establishments, and the population by way of redistribution | From the State Budget (excluding pensions, benefits, and grants) | From State insurance | From social insurance (excluding pensions and benefits) | From the credit systems | From savings banks | Received from the sale of services | Wages and salaries received by the population from nonproductive organizations | Pensions, benefits, and grants | Received directly from productive enterprises to maintain nonproductive branches. | Material benefits received by the population from nonproductive organizations | Decrease in cash in hand | Increase of creditor liabilities | Balance of redistribution | of which temporary redistribution | Total social product utilized | Compensation for productive expenditures on materials | Consumption | Increase in fixed assets | Increase in material working capital, reserves, and consumer stocks | Total accumulation | Losses from the social product and compensation of losses from funds |
| 23 | 24 | 25 | 26 | 27 | 28 | 29 | 30 | 31 | 32 | 33 | 34 | 35 | 36 | 37 | 38 | 39 | 40 | 41 | 42 | 43 | 44 |
| | | | x | | | x | x | x | x | x | | | | | | | x | | | | |
| | | | x | | | x | x | x | x | x | | | | | | | x | | | | |
| | | | x | | | x | x | x | x | x | | | | | | | x | | | | |
| | | | | | | | | | | | | | | | | | | | | | |
| | | | x | x | | x | x | x | x | x | x | | | | | | x | | | | |
| | | | x | x | | x | x | x | x | x | x | | | | | | x | | | | |
| | | | x | | | x | x | x | x | x | | | | | | | x | | | | |
| | | | | | | | | | | | | | | | | | | | | | |
| | | | x | | | x | x | x | x | x | | | | | | | x | | | | |
| | | | x | | | x | x | x | x | x | | | | | | | x | | | | |
| | | | x | | | x | x | x | x | x | | | | | | | x | | | | |
| | | | x | | | x | x | x | x | x | | | | | | | x | | | | |
| | | | x | | | x | x | x | x | x | | | | | | | x | | | | |
| | | | | | | | | | | | | | | | | | | | | | |
| | | | x | | | x | x | x | x | x | | | | | | | x | | | | |

## Table 5-2 (continued)

| | 1 | 2 | 3 | 4 | 5 | 6 | 7 | 8 | 9 | 10 | 11 | 12 | 13 | 14 | 15 | 16 | 17 | 18 | 19 | 20 | 21 | 22 |
|---|---|---|---|---|---|---|---|---|---|---|---|---|---|---|---|---|---|---|---|---|---|---|
| B. *Nonproductive establishments and organizations* | | | | | | | | | | | | | | | | | | | | | | |
| a) Cultural and communal establishments and organizations serving the population | X | X | X | X | X | X | X | X | X | X | | | | | | | | | X | | | |
| including: | | | | | | | | | | | | | | | | | | | | | | |
| 1) Education and the arts | X | X | X | X | X | X | X | X | X | X | | | | | | | | | X | | | |
| 2) Health services | X | X | X | X | X | X | X | X | X | X | | | | | | | | | X | | | |
| 3) Housing—communal and other enterprises and organizations providing personal services to the population | X | X | X | X | X | X | X | X | X | X | | | | | | | | | X | | | |
| b) Scientific establishments and organizations | X | X | X | X | X | X | X | X | X | X | | | | | | | | | X | | | |
| c) General administration and defense | X | X | X | X | X | X | X | X | X | X | | | | | | | | | X | | | |
| including: | | | | | | | | | | | | | | | | | | | | | | |
| 1) Public bodies | X | X | X | X | X | X | X | X | X | X | | | | | | | | | X | | | |
| 2) General administration and defense | X | X | X | X | X | X | X | X | X | X | | | | | | | | | X | | | |
| Total for nonproductive establishments and organizations | X | X | X | X | X | X | X | X | X | X | | | | | | | | | X | | | |
| of which: | | | | | | | | | | | | | | | | | | | | | | |
| a) State institutions and organizations | X | X | X | X | X | X | X | X | X | X | | | | | | | | | X | | | |
| b) Cooperative establishments and organizations | X | X | X | X | X | X | X | X | X | X | | | | | | | | | X | | | |
| C. *Total population* | X | X | X | X | X | X | X | X | | X | | | | | | | | X | X | X | | |
| of whom: | | | | | | | | | | | | | | | | | | | | | | |
| a) Workers and employees | X | X | X | X | X | X | X | X | | X | | | | | | | | X | X | X | | |
| b) Peasants | X | X | X | X | X | X | X | X | | X | | | | | | | | X | X | X | | |
| Total for the national economy | | | | | | | | | X | X | | | | | | | | | | | | |
| Additional receipts from outside sources | X | X | X | X | X | X | X | X | X | | | | X | X | X | X | X | X | X | | X | X |
| Total, including receipts from outside sources | | | | | | | | | X | | | | | | | | | | | | | |

Source: V. A. Sobol', *Ocherki po voprosam balansa narodnogo khoziastva,* Moscow 1960, Table 5.

items, etc. Finally, columns 38-44 show final distribution of social product and national income for the year in terms of consumption, capital investment, changes in reserves, etc.

The rows (lines) are broken down by: A. Enterprises engaged in material production; B. Nonproductive establishments; and C. Population. Both A and B include two cross classifications.

Relevant "military" items are to be found, at least, in rows B, c and B, c, 2 (general administration and defense), and possibly some

**Table 5-2 (continued)**

| 23 | 24 | 25 | 26 | 27 | 28 | 29 | 30 | 31 | 32 | 33 | 34 | 35 | 36 | 37 | 38 | 39 | 40 | 41 | 42 | 43 | 44 |
|----|----|----|----|----|----|----|----|----|----|----|----|----|----|----|----|----|----|----|----|----|----|
|  |  |  |  |  |  |  |  |  |  |  |  |  |  |  |  |  |  |  |  |  |  |
|  |  |  |  |  |  |  | x | x |  | x |  |  |  |  |  | x |  |  |  |  |  |
|  |  |  |  |  |  |  | x | x |  | x |  |  |  |  |  | x |  |  |  |  |  |
|  |  |  |  |  |  |  | x | x |  | x |  |  |  |  |  | x |  |  |  |  |  |
|  |  |  |  |  |  |  | x | x |  | x |  |  |  |  |  | x |  |  |  |  |  |
|  |  |  |  |  |  |  | x | x |  | x |  |  |  |  |  | x |  |  |  |  |  |
|  |  |  |  |  |  |  | x | x |  | x |  |  |  |  |  | x |  |  |  |  |  |
|  |  |  |  |  |  |  | x | x |  | x |  |  |  |  |  | x |  |  |  |  |  |
|  |  |  |  |  |  |  | x | x |  | x |  |  |  |  |  | x |  |  |  |  |  |
|  |  |  |  |  |  |  | x | x |  | x |  |  |  |  |  | x |  |  |  |  |  |
|  |  |  |  |  |  |  | x | x |  | x |  |  |  |  |  | x |  |  |  |  |  |
|  |  |  |  |  |  |  | x | x |  | x |  |  |  |  |  | x |  |  |  |  |  |
|  |  |  | x |  |  |  |  |  | x |  |  |  |  |  |  | x |  |  |  |  |  |
|  |  |  | x |  |  |  |  |  | x |  |  |  |  |  |  | x |  |  |  |  |  |
|  |  |  | x |  |  |  |  |  | x |  |  |  |  |  |  | x |  |  |  |  |  |
|  |  |  |  |  |  |  |  |  |  |  |  |  |  |  |  |  |  |  |  |  |  |
| x | x | x | x | x | x | x | x | x | x | x | x | x | x | x | x | x | x | x | x | x | x |
|  |  |  |  |  |  |  |  |  |  |  |  |  |  |  |  |  |  |  |  |  |  |

may also be included in A, I, a; A, II, 1 and 4; and in C. The following columns include military items: columns 18 and 30 (wages paid by nonproductive organizations, which includes military pay); columns 20 and 33 (direct support of the population, which includes military subsistence); column 24 (outlays of the State Budget); and column 42, which includes reserves.

As noted above, all budget revenue and expenditure are included in this table. Budget revenue appears in column 12 divided not by type of payment, as in the budget, but by the sector paying the revenue (industrial enterprise, social organization, population, etc.). This may aid in making rough cross checks. Expenditures presented in column 24 follow much the same lines as the budget. The banking system is included by virtue of columns 15, 16, 21, 22, 27, 28, 34, and 35.

Despite the apparent promise of the Financial Balance as a possible source of cross checks, it is admittedly very difficult to figure out how it might be used when it is presented only in the abstract (without any data whatsoever, even data "cooked up" for illustrative purposes). To compound the difficulties, the basic methodology is not revealed and the various categories and their interrelationships pose many puzzles. To present a few:

1. What is the nature of the cell entitled "Received from outside sources"[1] in which column 10 and the bottom row of the matrix meet?

2. What is the meaning of column 44 ("Losses from the social product. . .")?

3. What precisely are the relationships between the Soviet national income categories, listed in column 1 (social product produced), column 2 (value of means of production transferred to the product), and column 8 (total national income)?

4. Column 12 is "To the state Budget" and column 16 is "To the savings banks." Since the savings banks' receipts largely go into the budget, does this arrangement imply a disaggregation? Or do the savings banks receipts eventually get into the budget in some unspecified way? There does not seem to be any row in which this could happen. If these funds do not get into the budget in the Financial Balance, then what is the meaning of column 24 ("From the State Budget"), since it excludes part of the budget's receipts? And how can one allocate directly "From savings banks" (column 28) to the various sectors of the economy when this is in fact done via the mediation of the budget? The problem with regard to "social insurance" is similar.

5. How is the revenue of budget institutions treated? If such revenue goes directly to the budget, it must be listed under column 12, but if it is nonbudgetary (vnebiudzhetnye) it may be included

---

[1]Possibly "Received from outside sources" is "net imports" and "Losses from the social product" is "net exports." Dr. Becker informs me that the latter are "accidental damage to and destruction of fixed and working capital."

in column 29, revenue from the sale of services. But what if it is sale of goods (e.g., books by publishers)?

There are many other puzzles, but presumably these could be cleared up if and when there were an agreement to make the Financial Balance available.

Granting the difficulties, we present a few illustrations of possible useful cross relationships of the Balance. It should be noted that because of the many types of aggregate balances which are presented, verification of "separate secret accounts" might be easier to uncover than a hiding of military expenditures under other expenditure categories; nevertheless, some checks regarding the latter also seem possible.

Suppose that some military expenditures are put into secret accounts along with an equivalent amount of budget revenue. (In this example, some guesswork regarding the meaning of categories is necessary. References to aggregate rows and columns should usually be taken to refer to one of the subcategories.) The following adjustments would have to be made in the Financial Balance. The amount in column 7 ("Fund for the satisfaction of social needs") with both A, I and A, II would have to be commensurately reduced. But presumably, the total of column 7 should be included in column 11, rows A, I and A, II and column 23, row B. (This latter cell might be entitled "total contribution by nonproductive establishments and organizations.") Here, presumably the reduction would be in B, c (general administration and defense). Furthermore, if the reduction represented military pay, row C (population) would have to be adjusted, since its payments to the budget in the form of taxes (column 12) and its receipts in the form of military pay (columns 18 and 30) and possibly "Material benefits supplied to (received by) the population from nonproductive organizations" (columns 20 and 33) would have been reduced. In addition, many totals would have to be adjusted downward: national income (column 8), columns 36, 38, and others. If the reduction represented military procurement, other corresponding changes would have to be made.

Suppose now our second method of masking clandestine expenditures is practiced: assume that expenditures for defense are put, say, in the FNE residual. This would reduce row B, c (general administration and defense) and this reduction would have to be reflected in one or more columns (say, 18, 20, 24) and an offsetting increase would have to show up in other rows and columns. For example, it would have to show up in one or more of the rows in A, II (as well as A, I). The corresponding columns might be 41 (increase in fixed assets) and 43 (total accumulation) if the FNE functional category is "investment"; if subsidies, perhaps column 39 (compensation for productive expenditures on materials). It would also show up in column 24 (payments by the State Budget) and some A, II rows, whether it were investment or subsidy. If the amount hidden is procurement of tanks, it would be reflected in the cell where row A, II, 1 (industry) meets column 19 (direct contributions of productive branches for maintenance of nonproductive branches). And, of course, every time a cell in the matrix is changed, an alteration has to be made in the totals of which it is a subcategory.

To look at the Financial Balance in more general terms, perhaps the most important two interrelationships are the balance of income and expenditure of the population, and the balance of income and expenditure of enterprises and organizations. Thus the income of the population from wages, pensions, grants, sales of services, etc., must equal outlays including changes in savings and cash balances; and the income to enterprises from sales of products must be accounted for as outlays for wages, materials, amortization, payments to the budget, new investment from profits, and so forth. Any adjustment which affects one side of the balance must also affect the other.

It should be stressed again that nonbudget as well as budget sources are included in the Financial Balance, thereby making it more difficult to falsify by, say, using the retained profits of enterprises, or additions to currency in circulation, or other nonbudget sources of expenditure.

The Financial Balance will, of course, balance regardless of whether clandestine expenditures are masked or not. If falsification is attempted, the interrelationships within the Balance will naturally all be adjusted in the ways described above. The superiority of the Financial Balance relative to the budget for verification purposes is due to two factors. First, while clandestine expenditures in the budget usually imply a change in many other categories, they need not make these changes explicit. That is to say, falsification can be confined largely to the budget accounts. On the other hand, the ramifications of a falsification in the Financial Balance inevitably are wider because of the many interrelationships made explicit. Second, the Financial Balance contains many more categories which are functionally related to other independent aspects of the economy than does the budget, especially budget expenditures. (As we saw earlier, budget receipts also have this type of superiority, for verification purposes, over budget expenditures.) So long as the Soviets continue to publish large amounts of other economic data (retail trade turnover, rate of accumulation, price indexes, changes in savings deposits, wage bill, labor force, etc.), falsification on a large scale is difficult (because of the many items in the balance affected by the change of any single item and the interrelations of these with independent economic data). Furthermore, even if falsification were attempted, it would be much more dysfunctional internally in the case of the Financial Balance than it would be in the case of the budget, because the aggregates contained in the former are so much more important.

Despite all these interrelationships, we should not overstate our case. It is important to note that unless the changes made (amounts simulated) are significantly large, they will be undetectable because of the unavoidable error factor which accompanies (must be allowed for in) all verification procedures of the sort contemplated with Soviet economic data.

To sum up: If the Soviets provided Financial Balance tables with data and in somewhat more detail, particularly on military categories, falsification of military expenditures would be made more difficult for them. If they also provided, as with the budget, tables from the recent past, verification of arms reduction could be made with even more confidence. The numerous interrelationships provided by the above Financial Balance, when taken in conjunction with the budget and with other data currently available, make possible many more checks on arms reduction than does the provision of budgetary data presented in isolation. Needless to add, even with all these data, it would still undoubtedly be possible to hide military expenditures if the determination to do so were sufficiently great.[m]

---

[m]We have not examined in detail the various sub-balances which are drawn up as part of the compilation of the overall financial balances. Some of these sub-balances, for example the balance of incomes and expenditures of the population, would undoubtedly be useful for verification purposes.

# 6 Verification by Sampling

In the preceding chapters, an attempt has been made to spell out some approaches to verification based on the acquisition of additional data on budgetary expenditures and the like. It is possible that the Soviets may be reluctant to release additional aggregative information in the amounts necessary for verification. Furthermore, even with more information there are serious obstacles to the identification of clandestine military expenditures. Therefore, an alternative method of verification is proposed here, one which does not require the surrender of additional aggregative information, yet one which gives promise of providing as reliable a check on compliance with an arms reduction agreement as may be obtained. This method is based on sampling techniques. Before outlining the proposal, it is to be stressed that the writer is not particularly skilled in the use of sampling techniques, auditing procedures, and so forth. Therefore, the procedures proposed below may contain some obvious loopholes not envisioned by the writer, over and above problems which *are* posed here but not answered. They are nevertheless presented as they are, in the hopes that they will be suggestive. If it seems that the general approach may be fruitful, then competent statisticians, accountants, and auditors should be brought in to work out the details and close as many loopholes as possible.

Before proceeding further, it should be mentioned that the feasibility of the proposal is enhanced by two institutional features of the Soviet financial system. First, all enterprise and organizational (expenditure) accounts are centralized in the Gosbank and Stroibank, with all budget accounts centralized in the former. Second, almost all payments, except wages and salaries, are made by check, voucher, or other form of bank account transfer rather than in cash.

## A. Budget Expenditures

Assume that military expenditures are 17½ percent of total budgeted expenditures and that an agreement has been reached to reduce the former by 15 percent, bringing them down to approximately 15 percent of the total. Assume further that all military expenditures go through the budget and that there is a suspicion that some clandestine military expenditures may be hidden in residuals or in other explicit budget expenditure categories.

The verification procedure envisioned is to run a sample check of *all* checks, vouchers, and so forth made out in the Gosbank on the budget account. If the sample is random and the distribution "by size" of checks made out for defense is identical with the size distribution of nondefense checks, then a relatively small number of checks would need to be sampled to be able to determine, with a high degree of probability, the percentage that military expenditures are of the total budget expenditures. Before turning to the required size of the sample, it is worth considering that the size distributions of military and nonmilitary checks may be dissimilar. Whether or not this is the case may be difficult to ascertain. One method of check would be to run a sample of American budget expenditures and examine the size distribution of payments of the two populations. Another possibility would be to request the Russians to allow us to do the same with their budget expenditures for a given past year. In fact, of course, if an agreement were concluded which allowed sampling by both nations for the purposes under discussion, it would be clear after the first sample were taken whether or not the size distributions were similar. If the size distributions did differ significantly, then larger (than we suggest below) samples might be necessary or resort might be had to stratified samples. Other suggestions are made in this chapter for situations in which military checks are generally smaller or larger, respectively, than nonmilitary checks.

Assume now that size distribution of checks is no problem. How many checks are likely to be issued and how large must our sample be? There is no easy answer to the first question. There is some information available which suggests that the number of checks issued on behalf of the budget may be in the range of 50 to 500 million. On April 27, 1965, Secretary of Defense Robert S. McNamara said that the U.S. Defense Department writes 90 million checks a year (*New York Times*, April 28, 1965, p. 47). This suggests a figure of perhaps twice that number for our total federal budget. A Russian source (cited by Judy, 1967) has stated that the Gosbank processes 3.3 million documents every day, or over one billion annually. Not all of these documents are checks, of course, nor are all checks on behalf of the State Budget. Nevertheless, these two sources would seem to suggest similar orders of magnitude.

Let us turn to the second question: How large must the (random) sample be? Amazingly small! Even if the total number of checks issued approached infinity, one could be 99 percent "confident" that the distribution of the sample differed by no more than ½ percent of the actual distribution (which is expected to be .15/.85) by taking a sampling of only 27,592 checks. In other words, if the sample did indeed show a .15/.85 distribution, we could be 99 percent sure (with certain reservations discussed later on) that the Soviets had reduced their military expenditures from 17 ½ to at least 15 ½ percent. If the total number of checks issued had been, say, 200 million, then our sample would have amounted to about .014 percent of the checks, or only 1 check for (roughly) every 7,000 issued. This is not a very substantial "intrusion."

Table 6-1 indicates the size of samples required for a range of confidence levels and error limits, given an infinite number of checks and an expected distribution of .15/.85. The figures are almost identical with those which would result if we had assumed a check population of, say, 200 million.

The confidence level, and the possible error that would be considered appropriate, is a value judgment. It seems clear that a 1 percent error would probably be too large, given a total expected change of 2½ percent in the percentage of defense expenditures to total expenditures. To the writer, .5 percent would seem satisfactory, though .2 or .1 percent might be considered more appropriate by those who prefer to err on the safe side. A confidence level of something less than .999, say .99 or .95, would also seem entirely appropriate for the purpose. A confidence level of .95 means that 19 out of 20 samples will show a distribution within the range of expected error if the Soviets are not cheating. It also implies that if the Soviets are cheating, there is a good probability that they will be caught. They can hardly be expected to run such a risk of detection.

The actual risk they run of detection in the event of cheating can be ascertained from Table 6-2.[a] Using the same set of confidence

[a]This table measures one minus the Beta (or Type II) error as opposed to the Alpha (or Type I) error in the previous table. For various alternative hypotheses, we have here a measure of our ability to reject a false hypothesis—in this case, that the distribution is .15/.85. It is likewise a measure of the risk the USSR is running of our rejecting what they want us to accept, namely that the null hypothesis is .15/.85.

## Table 6-1
## Size of Required Sample[a]

| Confidence Level | (Size of error in percent) | | | |
|---|---|---|---|---|
| | .1% Error | .2% Error | .5% Error | 1.0% Error |
| .95 | 345,018 | 86,255 | 13,801 | 3,450 |
| .99 | 689,810 | 172,453 | 27,592 | 6,898 |
| .999 | 1,217,383 | 304,346 | 48,695 | 12,174 |

[a]Estimates assume an infinite number of payments and sample for one-tail error.

## Table 6-2
## Risk of Detection

| Confidence Levels (percent) | Alternative 1 $\pi a = 17.5$ | | | | Alternative 2 $\pi a = 17.0$ | | | |
|---|---|---|---|---|---|---|---|---|
| | (Error limits in percent) | | | | | | | |
| | .1 | .2 | .5 | 1.0 | .1 | .2 | .5 | 1.0 |
| 95 | ~1 | ~1 | ~1 | .9931 | ~1 | ~1 | ~1 | .95 |
| 99 | ~1 | ~1 | ~1 | ~1. | ~1 | ~1 | ~1 | .99 |
| 99.9 | ~1 | ~1 | ~1 | ~1. | ~1 | ~1 | ~1 | .999 |

| Confidence Levels (percent) | Alternative 3 $\pi a = 16.5$ | | | | Alternative 4 $\pi a = 16.0$ | | | |
|---|---|---|---|---|---|---|---|---|
| | (Error limits in percent) | | | | | | | |
| | .1 | .2 | .5 | 1.0 | .1 | .2 | .5 | 1.0 |
| 95 | ~1 | ~1 | ~1 | .7937 | ~1 | ~1 | .95 | .5 |
| 99 | ~1 | ~1 | ~1 | .877 | ~1 | ~1 | .99 | .5 |
| 99.9 | ~1 | ~1 | ~1 | .9394 | ~1 | ~1 | .999 | .5 |

| Confidence Levels (percent) | Alternative 5 $\pi a = 15.5$ | | | |
|---|---|---|---|---|
| | (Error limits in percent) | | | |
| | .1 | .2 | .5 | 1.0 |
| 95 | ~1 | .993 | .5 | .206 |
| 99 | ~1 | ~1. | .5 | .123 |
| 99.9 | ~1 | ~1. | .5 | .062 |

levels, error limits, and (therefore) sample sizes as the previous table, this table tells us the risk of detection the Soviets run under five alternative hypotheses ranging from no actual reduction of defense expenditures by the Soviets (.175/.825) to a reduction equal to 80 percent of that agreed upon (.155/.845), the agreed distribution being .15/.85.

Suppose we think that the Soviets have not reduced their defense expenditures at all but are maintaining them at 17.5 percent of the budget. Given this hypothesis, we might say to ourselves: What is the chance of detection assuming 99 percent confidence levels with error limits of .5 or 1.0 percent respectively? These large error limits would be admissible in this case, since we are testing for a large deception of 2.5 percent. From the table, it is clear that the probability of detection would approach 100 percent with samples of 27,592 and 6,898 respectively.

Let us take another example. Suppose our hypothesis is that the Soviets have reduced their defense expenditures from 17.5 to 16 percent, rather than to 15 percent, of the budget. This is a smaller degree of cheating and our error limits would have to be more refined. Thus, even though we would have, with a sample of 6,898 checks, a 50 percent chance of detecting cheating, this would not be meaningful because it is based on a 1 percent error limit, which raises the possibility of misinterpreting compliance by the Russians ($16 - 1 = 15$) as cheating. There is another way to look at it: it does not make much sense to test for cheating amounting to 1 percent of budget expenditures with a test that admits an error factor of 1 percent. Under these circumstances, a .5 percent error might be admissible and, as the table indicates, with a 99 percent confidence level, detection is 99 percent certain given a sample of 27,592 checks. Approximately 100 percent certainty can be obtained with smaller error limits but the samples required are much larger.

Suppose now that we suspect the Soviets of having reduced their military expenditures by 80 percent of the amount agreed upon, but of cheating on the last 20 percent, or by .5 percent of budget expenditures. In this case, by similar reasoning, the error limit would have to be less than .5 percent, say .2 or .1 percent. In order to be almost 100 percent certain of detecting cheating here, given the same confidence limits (99 percent), much larger samples are required, 172,453 and 689,810 respectively. In other words, since the cheating suspected is so much smaller, the power of the test is reduced and much larger samples are required to obtain the same degree of certainty. But it is important to note here that one would be much less concerned by cheating of only 20 percent—i.e., 80 percent compliance with an arms reduction agreement might be considered pretty good.

Under these circumstances, one might be willing to reduce the power of the test and accept a 95 percent confidence level or even a slightly larger error limit (say .3 or .35 percent) and less than a 100 percent chance of detection. All these changes would reduce the size of sample required. Finally, in connection with the near 100 percent probability-of-detection criterion, it is perhaps worth noting that, while we might feel that it is necessary to ensure a very high probability of detection, it is important to note that from the Soviet point of view it might not be considered feasible to cheat even if the probability of detection were very low, say 1 chance out of 3.

The upshot of all this discussion is that a very small sample of checks indeed is required to make the risk of being caught cheating unbearably high.

Let us turn now to details regarding how the sample is to be used and to some of the problems that arise in using this technique.

The percentage of defense expenditures to the total could in theory be obtained from a sample on the basis *either* of "numbers" of checks made out on behalf of defense, relative to nondefense, *or* on the basis of "sums of values." The numbers approach has a major weakness in that the Soviets could easily bias the results by making some nondefense payments in many checks of small denominations. This problem is avoided by the "sums of values" approach.

A related difficulty is posed if, for camouflage purposes, the Soviets make some of their defense expenditures in huge aggregated amounts. If there were only two or three such and they totaled, say, one-third of military expenditures, it would be unlikely that they would be picked up in a random sample. (The fear of their being selected in the random sample might inhibit the use of such a device, however.) This difficulty could be avoided if, somehow, the Soviets could be required to submit their checks in the form of cumulated totals. The application of random numbers to these totals would have a greater probability of picking up large checks than small checks, thereby preventing this device from being used as a technique for cheating.[b]

[b]Suppose the total population of checks issued is 10 as shown in order of issuance in the following table along with cumulative totals:

| Check Amounts | Cumulative Total |
| --- | --- |
| | 0 |
| 1 | 1 |
| 2 | 3 |

Another verification problem is raised if the Soviets begin to make an increasing percentage of military payments in cash. In fact, if the method envisioned is to be successful, it will be necessary for the Soviets to make all budget payments, at least preliminarily, by check. That is to say, even if soldiers (for example) are paid in cash, a voucher will be made out originally, and made available to auditors, indicating the transfer of cash.

Another important way in which the Soviets would have to cooperate if the proposed system were to work would be to organize their accounts and payment systems in such a way that it would be possible to devise a means of taking a random sample of the checks. For example, the checks would have to be serialized in some systematic way. Whatever the method chosen, it would have to be random with respect to institutions doing the paying. One method, for example, would be to number checks using IBM-type clocks, which would stamp on a check the date, hour, minute, second, and perhaps fraction of a second of the payment. Other methods undoubtedly can be devised.

There is at least one more prerequisite if the proposed sampling system is to work satisfactorily. (A problem which remains unsolved, as yet, is presented in Section C of this chapter.) One of the problems posed above was that the Soviets might hide military payments under other categories. In order to prevent this from happening at the level of individual payments, the U.S. auditors would have to be allowed the privilege of rigorously identifying any check which has been pulled in the random sample—much in the way a bank or other auditor would be allowed to do in this country—to make sure the check accurately represents the payment for which it is ostensibly made. In other words, this would enable us to detect any attempt to call, say, a tank a tractor. Suppose, for example, that in order to simulate compliance with the disarmament

| | |
|---|---|
| 20 | 23 |
| 100 | 123 |
| 200 | 323 |
| 300 | 623 |
| 500 | 1,123 |
| 50 | 1,173 |
| 35 | 1,208 |
| 200 | 1,408 |

Suppose the first random number drawn is .67302. Multiplying .67302 by 1,408 gives approximately 946. Thus the first check picked in our sample would be the $500 check. And so forth.

agreement, the Soviets falsified the nature of 15 percent of their defense checks (implying a 15 percent reduction in armament expenditure). With defense, in our example, amounting to 15 percent of the budget, falsified checks would amount to roughly 2¼ percent of total budget expenditures and, presumably, they should show up as roughly 2¼ percent of the checks in the sample. In order to be quite certain that the Soviets are not falsifying checks in the way indicated, it would not be necessary to rigorously identify (audit fully) all checks, but only a small percentage of those in our sample via a random sample. The number of checks to be audited would depend on the size of the sample and the percentage of falsification that one wished to detect. For example, suppose our original sample (our present universe) were 20,000 checks. If the Soviets were simulating a reduction in defense expenditures which amounted to 2 percent of the total budget, then the original sample should contain some 400 falsified checks. One could be 95 percent certain of turning up at least one falsified check out of the 400 by taking a random sample of 1,370 checks (out of 20,000) for rigorous identification. A sample of 3,000 checks would yield a probability of 99.9 percent of finding a falsified check. If the degree of simulation being attempted were on a smaller scale, say ½ percent of the budget, then the sample required for a rigorous audit would have to be correspondingly larger. To have a 99 percent probability of finding *one* false check, one would have to rigorously audit about 7,400 checks; a 99.9 percent probability would require the audit of 10,000 checks; 5,200 checks would suffice for 95 percent probability.

It is perhaps worth noting that audits of this sort would be quite costly and time-consuming and, even though the number of checks to be audited would not be large in the relative sense, they would have a high annoyance value. While there is little that can be done to reduce the annoyance value, the costliness would be small compared to the savings to either nation which would result from genuine arms reduction.

Finally, it is worth noting that the procedures sketched above would enable us not only to estimate the percentage of defense to total budget expenditures and to detect the possibility of falsification of category; they would also enable us to estimate the percent of subsidies (as well as "unconventional budgetary practices") in the budget and the possibility that these might be used to simulate reduction of budgeted military expenditures.

## B. Total Expenditures: Budget Plus Nonbudget

In Chapter 4 we outlined several ways in which military expenditures might by-pass the budget. This does not create any new problems of principle, nor does it create insurmountable practical problems. The problem, under these circumstances, shifts from taking a random sample of the budget accounts in the Gosbank to taking a random sample of all payments made through the Gosbank and Stroibank. This would expand the total number of payments substantially, because the population of checks would now encompass not only final products purchased through the budget but also intermediate products purchased by enterprises and organizations and also payroll.

It might be more difficult to gain permission to perform a verification along these lines, for two reasons. First, it would be much more comprehensive, thereby substantially raising the costs of preparation, not to speak of the annoyance factor. Second, a sample check of what would amount to practically all enterprise and organizational transactions in the economy would put the auditing nation in a position to reconstruct with a high degree of accuracy the structure of the Soviet economy. In fact, the auditor might obtain more information about the Soviet economy from such a sample check than it would from the publication of a large number of additional time series of the type required for verification in Chapter 5.

## C. Separate Secret Accounts Again

A major stumbling block to verification in Chapter 5 was the possibility that the Soviets would hide accounts—establish a set of secret accounts outside the budget, Gosbank, and Stroibank. Some approaches to this problem were suggested in Chapter 5 but they were far from foolproof. The separate secret accounts are also a serious stumbling block to the successful use of the sampling techniques outlined above. If accounts are taken entirely out of the regular financial channels, then the random sample is effectively by-passed.

In principle, there would seem to be an approach to this problem which should work; in practice, the approach appears unworkable. Basically, the approach is to work back from the physical military goods and services (including labor services) to the accounts in the Gosbank and Stroibank. If a random sample could be taken of all the things that can be classified as military goods and services (pay of one soldier in Moscow, a tank produced in Kharkov, a missile, etc.) and each item is followed back in the accounts to be sure that it was originally financed out of the defense item in the budget, with a fairly small sample one could tell with a high degree of certainty whether or not the accounts had been tampered with. If items turned out to have been classified in a "residual" or under "FNE—investment," or do not appear in any known account (separate secret accounts), then the nature of the "tampering" would be evident.

An important reason why this system might work, in principle, is that the items which the Soviets might choose to mask from the budget would not necessarily be the items (such as missiles) which they would want to mask physically. The budgeted military expenditures might well be reduced, for example, by simply taking out of the budget the wages of workers building a military airfield near Leningrad. So long as missiles and other sensitive material are hidden physically, there is no need to hide them in secret accounts (if access to the budget accounts is limited).

There are at least two problems which appear to make this approach unfeasible. First, if this type of verification were used, the Soviets might very quickly adapt themselves to avoid detection by developing a correspondence between those items which are physically hidden from foreigners and those which are hidden in the accounts. If they did this, and if sensitive material were successfully hidden physically, which should not be difficult, then the secret accounts could not be detected by this method.

Second, and more fundamental, I have not been able to think of any way of getting a random sample of the physical counterpart of military expenditure. Even if one leaves aside the question of sensitive items which are physically hidden, how to take a random sample of the remainder poses, to my mind, very difficult problems. There may be other approaches to this problem, however, and perhaps qualified statisticians can come up with answers.[c]

---

[c]Some cause for optimism is provided by the sampling exploits of British and American statisticians during World War II. They were able to estimate German war production as accurately as, and more quickly than, the Germans themselves (postwar studies showed) by the use of such information as serial numbers on captured equipment, train schedules, and so forth. See, for example Wallis and Roberts (1956, p. 20).

## D. Concluding Comment

It should be explicitly noted that an approach similar to the one presented above might be used, not as an independent means of verification, but as a complement to verification based on the submission of additional data as presented in Chapter 5.

# Appendix:
# Soviet Military Outlays and
# the Problem of Residuals in
# the USSR State Budget

## A. General Comments

The existence of large unspecified residuals in the USSR State Budget has attracted the attention of several Western economists studying the Soviet economy. Residuals usually consist of a number of small miscellaneous items, but in the USSR State Budget, in several instances, the residuals are too large to be satisfactorily explained in this manner.

Analysis of the residuals is made difficult by the vagueness and paucity of Soviet budget statistics. Generally, only the totals of the major budget categories are published by the Soviet government, giving rise to a great deal of speculation concerning what actually may or may not be included. While much supplementary information is published from time to time in various statistical compilations, these appear at irregular intervals and do not follow any consistent pattern. Often they raise more questions than they answer.

In Chapters 2 and 3, we discussed what is known about the content of the explicit defense expenditure item in the State Budget and also presented some of the more salient features of the budget residuals. In the following sections an attempt is made to summarize and evaluate in more detail the work that has been done by U.S. economists studying Soviet budgeted military outlays. No independent systematic study has been made of the Soviet sources themselves. Moreover, the question of the validity of Soviet budget statistics is not raised again—the reader is referred to the discussion in Chapter 3.

## B. Financing the National Economy Residuals

The obvious place in the budget to look for hidden military outlays is the Financing the National Economy (FNE) category: first, because it is the largest single budget category (amounting to almost 50 percent of total outlay); second, because large amounts of the outlays are unexplained; and third, because the defense industry is financed under this category. FNE may be broken down by sector of the economy (industry, agriculture, etc.), by end-use (investment, working capital, etc.), or by various combinations of these two. Furthermore, it is sometimes instructive to view the outlays from the All-Union Budget separately from the budgets of the Republics on the theory that outlays of military significance most likely lie in the All-Union Budget.

There are three items of potentially military significance usually assumed to be in the FNE category.

*Operational Grants to the Defense Industry.* The most important types are outlays for development, testing, and mastery of production of new weapons, and subsidies to cover losses of the defense industry. (Investment in the defense industry, financed from this category, presents a separate problem, related to the general question of Soviet pricing discussed in Chapter 3, Section E.)

*Additions to State Reserves.* We know that state reserves are financed from the FNE category and we know that, by definition, they include defense as well as other items. We also know from discussions of national income that state reserves are a significant item (5 to 6 percent) in the Soviet national income. It is tempting to assume that some portion of military supplies and hardware may be procured not by direct purchase by the Ministry of Defense but by purchase as state reserves. (This is discussed in Chapter 3, Section B.)

*Atomic Energy Programs.* Very little is known about the financing of Soviet atomic energy programs, but the administration apparently lies partly in the Ministry of Medium Machine Building and partly in the State Committee for Peaceful Uses of Atomic Energy. The former is definitely included in the FNE category and the latter probably is. The products and services encompassed by these programs seem to lend themselves to complete budget financing, and it is doubtful that goods or services are sold on any large scale to the Ministry of Defense or other Soviet organizations. Nonetheless, concrete evidence on this question is lacking and conclusions are pure conjecture.

Attention of most observers has been focused on the following four residuals. The first two are FNE residuals properly speaking, while the latter two are residuals within the industry section of the FNE category.

## 1. FNE Sector Residual

This residual is the easiest to calculate because most of the data are readily available. It is also perhaps the least satisfactory, because it leaves intact the most significant allocation—that to industry. Table A-1 shows the size of this residual for selected years since 1960 (figures for 1974 should be viewed with caution, because they are the planned amount and not strictly comparable to the earlier years).

The size of the FNE sector residual has increased dramatically in recent years, both in absolute terms and as a percentage of the total FNE allocation. As Table A-1 indicates, the residual increased from 4.5 billion rubles in 1960 to 15.8 billion rubles in 1970 and to 26.8 billion rubles planned for 1974.

The largest factor in this increase appears to consist of price-differential grants paid from the budget to keep retail food prices low. Since 1969, prices paid to agricultural producers for procurement of foodstuffs have increased sharply while retail prices have remained stable. This has necessitated large price-differential grants from the budget. Similar price adjustments on agricultural produce were made in the budgets of the 1950s.

Information recently published in the Soviet Union has made it possible to determine the general size of these budget payments. According to the best estimates available, outlays from the budget were 7.9 billion rubles in 1969, 14.3 billion rubles in 1970, and 16.0 billion rubles in the 1974 plan (see Krueger, 1974, pp. 63-65; also Semenov, 1974, pp. 37-47).

Although the price-differential grants in agriculture explain the large increase in the budget residual in recent years, many questions remain. Why was the residual as high as 7.8 billion rubles in 1965, a year when the price-differential grants from the budget were minimal? Why did the residual jump by 11 billion rubles, from a total of 15.8 in 1970 to 26.8 in 1974, when the price-differential grants appear to have increased by less than 2 billion rubles over the same period?

### Table A-1
### Expenditures of the State Budget of the USSR, Selected Years (billions of rubles)

| | 1960 | 1965 | 1970 | 1974 Plan[a] |
|---|---|---|---|---|
| 1. Financing the national economy | 34.1 | 44.9 | 74.6 | 95.1 |
| Industry and construction | 15.6 | 21.0 | 30.5 | 36.7 |
| Agriculture and procurements | 4.7 | 6.8 | 12.4 | 15.1 |
| Trade | 3.6 | 2.3 | 6.3 | (6.5)[b] |
| Transport and communications | 2.8 | 2.8 | 3.1 | 3.8 |
| Municipal economy | 3.2 | 4.2 | 6.5 | 6.2 |
| Other (FNE sector residual) | 4.2 | 7.8 | 15.8 | 26.8 |
| 2. Social-cultural measures | 24.9 | 38.2 | 55.9 | 70.3 |
| Education | 8.0 | 13.2 | 18.2 ⎫ | 31.2 |
| Science | 2.3 | 4.3 | 6.5 ⎬ | |
| Health and physical culture | 4.8 | 6.7 | 9.3 | 10.7 |
| Social welfare | 9.8 | 14.0 | 21.8 | 28.4 |
| 3. Defense | 9.3 | 12.8 | 17.9 | 17.6 |
| 4. Administration | 1.1 | 1.3 | 1.7 | 1.8 |
| 5. Other (General Expenditures residual) | 3.7 | 4.4 | 4.5 | 9.3[a] |
| Total expenditure | 73.1 | 101.6 | 154.6 | 194.1 |

[a]Not strictly comparable to earlier years because the figures are planned amounts, not actual.
[b]Estimate.

Sources: USSR, *Gosudarstvennyi Biudzhet SSSR*, 1966, 1966-1970; *Finansy SSSR*, No. 1, 1974, pp. 4, 9, 13.

Any conclusion to be drawn from an analysis of the FNE sector residual depends on the accuracy of the data on price-differential grants. The Soviet government has been extremely reluctant in the post-World War II period to publish precise data on price differentials which can be directly related to budget categories.[a] Therefore, the use of this residual as an indicator of either the size or the direction of Soviet military outlays is severely limited unless more data are made available.

Very little is known about other miscellaneous items which may be included in this residual. They include the following:

[a]It is generally assumed that these price-differential grants are paid out of the FNE category because they are similar in nature to other outlays (state subsidies, operational expenditures) which are known to be paid from FNE, because procurement in general is financed under this category, and because the residual is in all years large enough to include it. However, discussions of the procedure in Soviet sources do not specify the budget category involved and in the 1953-1954 period there was evidence that these grants were paid out of the General Expenditures residual (Nove, 1954).

**Gold Purchases.** Impossible to estimate, but probably small. One estimate gives the figure of .1 billion rubles for the years 1955-1962 (Becker, 1964, p. 28).

**Geologic Survey, Prospecting.** Again, impossible to estimate, but probably small.

**Atomic Energy Outlays.** These may be wholly or in part in this residual or they may be included under the industry category. No information on the cost of atomic energy programs is available in Soviet sources, but a recent study estimating Soviet costs on the basis of U.S. outlays put the allocation for atomic energy programs at 1 billion rubles annually (SIPRI, 1974).

**State Reserves.** No information is available on the magnitude of outlays for State Reserves. This is a functional category, similar to investment, so that industrial reserves are included under industry and agricultural reserves are included under agriculture. The possibility that some military procurement is included in State Reserves is discussed above (Chapter 3, Section B). If military procurement is included in State Reserves, it could come under the industry allocation or in the residual, or perhaps partly in both, depending on the nature of the items procured.

**Other Possible Items.** Nothing is known about budget financing of "foreign economic relations," i.e., military aid, and technical and economic assistance to foreign nations. Nor do we know about funding for civil defense. These items may be included here, or they may be part of the General Expenditures residual. In either event, they are probably not large.

In summary, the usefulness of the FNE sector residual is limited because it consists of one large item and several small items which may fluctuate widely and which cannot be estimated with any degree of accuracy on the basis of currently available information. Moreover, defense outlays may be placed not in this residual but in the industry category. Nevertheless, in the case of an arms reduction agreement this residual should be examined carefully as a possible source of hidden military outlay.

## 2. FNE End-Use Residual.

This breakdown of the FNE category is theoretically more useful because it may include possible military items under the industry category. But as a practical matter, the necessary data are almost completely lacking and it is necessary to rely upon estimates of varying validity (see Table A-2). The items which have to be estimated here are as follows:

**Investment.** This generally accounts for about 50 percent of the total. Seldom do the Soviets provide the exact figure for financing capital investment from the budget FNE category. However, enough information on the volume of investment is available to permit fairly good estimates.

**Increases in Working Capital Norms.** We have the plan figures for this for most years.

**MTS Grant and Outlays for Planning Design Bureaus.** We have figures for these two items. With the abolition of the MTS, this grant disappeared.

**Price-Differential Grants.** Foreign trade grants have been estimated on the basis of scattered data. They were presumably wiped out as a result of the 1961 revaluation of the ruble. Price-differential grants for agricultural produce were discussed above.

**Subsidies.** These are extremely difficult to estimate. Included are direct subsidies to cover operating losses in some industries as well as other types of budget grants for operational expenditures. Recent increases in wholesale prices were designed to increase profits and wipe out subsidies. It is believed that some subsidy payments are still made from the budget, but there is no way to estimate their magnitude.

**Other Items.** The resulting residual includes gold purchase, outlays for geological prospecting, starting outlays for new enterprises, developmental outlays, and purchases for State Reserves. These miscellaneous items make up a large portion of the total category,

**Table A-2**
**USSR State Budget Outlays on the National Economy, by End-Use, 1956 and 1960 (billions of rubles)**

|                                      | 1956    | 1960 Plan  |
|--------------------------------------|---------|------------|
| Investment                           | 12.43   | (16.69)    |
| Capital repair                       | (.40)   | (.50)      |
| Expansion of working capital norms   | .38     | .73        |
| Subsidies                            | (1.20)  | (1.20)     |
| MTS grant                            | 2.00    | negligible |
| Price differential grants            |         |            |
|   Foreign trade            | (1.10)  | (1.90)     |
|   Agricultural procurement | (.60)   | negligible |
| Planning design bureaus              | .49     | .62        |
| Other (residual)                     | (5.92)  | (11.21)    |
| Total                                | 24.52   | 32.85      |

Source: U.S., CIA, *The 1960 Soviet Budget,* p. 20. Figures in parentheses are estimates.

for example about 25 percent of the total in 1956 and almost one-third in the 1960 plan. More information about the items in this residual is clearly desirable.

No attempt has been made to calculate an FNE end-use residual since 1960 because of the large uncertainties involved. However, it can be noted that investment, the largest component in the end-use category, has been increasing at a slower rate than the total FNE category, resulting in an increase in the residual both in ruble terms and as a percent of the total. For example, in the 1974 plan budget, centralized investments from the budget are 37 billion rubles out of the total FNE allocation of 95.1 billion rubles. As with FNE sector residual, the explanation for this increase appears to be the large price-differential grants to cover the higher costs of procurement of agricultural produce, estimated at 16.9 billion rubles in the 1974 plan.

## 3. Industry-Construction End-Use Residual

This calculation is based on the assumption that, since the defense industry is financed under the industry subcategory of FNE, this is

**Table A-3**
**Industry-Construction Residual of the USSR State Budget, 1955-1962 (billions of rubles)**

| | 1955 | 1956 | 1957 | 1958 | 1959 | 1960 | 1961 Plan | 1962 Plan |
|---|---|---|---|---|---|---|---|---|
| Industry-construction total | 11.02 | 12.82 | 13.08 | (14.57) | (16.01) | (17.95) | 16.1 | 14.8 |
| Investment | 7.28 | 8.00 | (8.52) | (9.18) | (9.67) | (10.40) | Not available | |
| Increase in working capital | (.39) | (.18) | (.32) | (.31) | (.17) | (.40) | | |
| Design bureaus | .45 | .50 | .52 | .56 | .60 | 0 | | |
| Research and development | (.50) | (.50) | (.40) | (.30) | (.20) | 0 | | |
| Subsidies paid from budget | (1.06) | (1.06) | (.56) | (1.20) | (1.80) | (3.00) | | |
| Other (residual) | (1.34) | (2.58) | (2.76) | (3.02) | (3.57) | (4.15) | | |

Source: U.S., CIA, *The Soviet Budget for 1962*, p. 24. Figures in parentheses are estimates.

the logical place to look for hidden military outlays. This breakdown is similar to the previous one except that only the industry portion of the various items is included. Thus it involves the same, or more, uncertainty in estimates of the various component items (see Table A-3).

Again, this residual would be valuable if it was a firm figure and not a guess. On the other hand, there is no doubt that this category is growing extremely rapidly, and the total is growing more rapidly than the major component part, investment. This means that subsidies or operational grants to industry are increasing rapidly, but there is no way of knowing how much of this is granted to the defense industry (perhaps in the form of reimbursement for development of new models, perhaps for subsidies, perhaps for purchase of output for State Reserves) and how much is used in civilian industry.

## 4. Industry-Construction Allocation from the All-Union Budget

Interest centered on this allocation during the period of decentralization of industry in the USSR (1958-1960). At that time, although most industry was transferred to the jurisdiction of the Councils of the National Economy (*sovnarkhoz*) and thereby to the Republic budgets, substantial amounts of money continued to be expended on industry out of the All-Union Budget (see Table A-4). It was argued at that time that the industry remaining under All-Union financing probably had some military significance.

There is no reason to assume that All-Union financing of industry is limited to the military sector only, or that it consists of hidden military spending as distinct from investment in the defense industry. In any event, the recentralization of financing of industry since the mid-1960s has reduced the significance of the All-Union allocation to industry as an indicator of activity in the defense sector.

## C. The Budget General Expenditure Residual

This figure is derived by subtracting the known budget categories (Financing the National Economy, Social-Culture, Defense, Administration) from total budget expenditure (see Table A-1). This

## Table A-4
## USSR State Budget Outlays to Industry by All-Union and Republic Budget

|      | All-Union Budget | Republic Budgets | Total State Budget |
|------|------------------|------------------|--------------------|
| 1955 | 8.8              | 2.2              | 11.0               |
| 1958 | 3.3              | 9.8              | 13.1               |
| 1960 | 4.0              | 11.6             | 15.6               |
| 1965 | 7.9              | 13.1             | 21.0               |
| 1970 | 22.7             | 7.8              | 30.5               |

Source: USSR, *Gosudarstvennyi Biudzhet SSSR*, 1962, pp. 18, 71; 1966-1970, pp. 25, 79.

category seems to be a miscellaneous catch-all for various items not included elsewhere. The Census Bureau study found "very little information" on these remaining groups (Gallik et al., 1968, pp. 76-77), but they are usually assumed to include the following:

**Accounts with Banks.** The extension of long-term credit by Soviet banks is made possible by budget grants. These sums are small, but they have been increasing in recent years. We do have scattered data on extension of long-term credit and thus may estimate the general size of these outlays.

**Internal Affairs and Security Agencies.** Support for the activities of these agencies, some of which are military in nature (e.g., border guards) has been in this residual. The Census Bureau study (Gallik et al., 1968, p. 75) found no mention of this group in recent years, which raises the possibility that it is no longer an independent category and its activities are now financed out of the administration category.

**Other.** Miscellaneous items here include payments to retail trade organizations for losses resulting from repricing inventories, some types of postal expenditures, local expenditures on street traffic regulation, and expenditure on the manufacture of medals and orders. Foreign aid and civil defense, if not included in the Financing the National Economy category, may be included here.

In conclusion, the General Expenditures residual does not appear to be a significant source of military outlays. The size of the residual, approximately 4 billion rubles, can be explained by budget outlays to long-term credit banks and other miscellaneous items.

However, it should be noted that the specific mechanism involved in credit extension in the Soviet economy is not clear from existing sources, and more information on this point would be helpful. Also more information is needed on the financing of border guards and other internal security functions which are normally categorized as defense outlay.

## D. Some Notes on Financing Scientific Research and Development

In searching for hidden military expenditures in the Soviet Union, many analysts have focused attention on the financing of scientific research and development in the military sphere. The explicit defense allocation in the USSR State Budget does not include any significant outlays for R&D. Although Soviet financial textbooks published in the 1950s include maintenance of scientific-research institutions as an item in the defense allocation, more recent editions of the textbooks omit mention of these institutions in discussions of the defense outlay. The only outlay for education in the defense allocation, according to recent information, is support for military academies and institutions (Gallik et al., 1968, p. 175).

Of course, some R&D may be charged to the cost of production of military hardware and thus included in the price paid for these goods by the Ministry of Defense. In this way, R&D would be indirectly included in the defense allocation. Not enough is known about the pricing of military hardware to make a definite conclusion about the amount of military R&D financed in this way.

The most important source of R&D funds in the Soviet Union is the allocation to science, listed under the Social-Cultural category of the USSR budget. These funds are used mainly to finance scientific research institutes. As might be expected in this period of rapidly expanding technology, these sums have been growing rapidly. Budget outlays for science have increased from 2.2 billion rubles in 1960 to 7.3 billion rubles in 1972 (USSR, Narkhoz, 1973, pp. 726-727).

It has generally been assumed in the West that a large component of the science allocation, perhaps one-half to two-thirds, should be considered military oriented. This assumption is based on the rapid rise in the science allocation and on the further (possibly question-begging) assumption that military R&D has been increasing more rapidly than nonmilitary.

Soviet sources on these questions are not without ambiguities. Nancy Nimitz, for example, who has made exhaustive studies of Soviet statistics on scientific R&D, concluded in a recent work that "the source likely to support most defense-space research, along with some civilian research, is the portion of the Budget allocation to science that comes directly from the All-union budget" (Nimitz, 1974, p. 14). On the other hand, there is some evidence that the science allocation excludes some military and space R&D.[b]

It should also be noted here that the Soviet series on science allocations over time differ. In some cases the reason for the difference is known and in other cases it is not. (For a summary discussion on this see Nolting, 1973, pp. 9-13).

Finally, the Soviet series on outlays for science do not encompass all the activity of the U.S. concept of RDT&E (research, development, testing, and evaluation). Costs of prototype development, testing, and assimilation into production are covered from other sources.

A wealth of material about R&D has been published in the Soviet Union in recent years. This material does not supply much information about the magnitude of civilian or of military R&D, but it does tell us a great deal about methods of financing.

In addition to the explicit allocation to science, budget sources of funds for R&D are:

1. *Education Allocation.* This category supports the Higher Educational Institutions (*VUZy*), which perform some scientific research. However, most of their science work is financed through the science allocation and therefore very little outlay for scientific research would come from this budget category.

2. *Financing the National Economy.* Under this category sums are expended to test new products and initiate production. One Soviet textbook on the budget, for example, states that "outlays for experimental work of scientific organizations, support for construction bureaus and factory laboratories, and laboratories of kombinats

---

[b]See Nolting (1973, p. 24) for a reference to an East German economist who implies that military R&D is excluded; and see the Soviet source Notkin (1973, p. 222) for a reference indicating that space outlays are excluded.

are included in the plan for the basic activity of the corresponding branch of the economy and are not included in outlays for financing culture" (Plotnikov, 1959, p. 300). Such "experimental" work, if financed by the budget, would be included in the Financing the National Economy category. Textbooks on financing the aircraft industry tell us that airplane experimental institutions are "gross budgetary" (i.e., all income goes into the budget and all outlay comes out of the budget). If this is true of other defense items also, the size could be considerable.

Organizational funds of various kinds are also used to finance scientific R&D. These funds include enterprise profits, amortization allowances, charges to the cost of production, and bank credit.

An official series on outlays to science including both budget and organizational funds is available for most recent years. In 1960, organization funds were 1.7 billion rubles and budget funds were 2.2 billion rubles, for a total of 3.9 billion rubles. In 1972, own funds had jumped to 7.1 billion rubles and budget funds were 7.3 billion, for a total of 14.4 billion (USSR, Narkhoz, 1973, pp. 726-727). Again, these figures do not include outlays for model development, testing, and "mastery of production."

There are several enterprise funds which may be used for R&D, including the Special Fund for Financing Scientific Research Work, the Fund for Assimilation of New Technology, the Fund for the Development of Production, and the Unified Fund for the Development of Science and Technology (see Nolting, 1973, pp. 28-34).

As explained above (Chapter 4, Section E), enterprise funds are not a source of hidden military outlay to the extent that they are included in the final price of the product sold. However, a problem arises if funds accumulated from the production of civilian goods are used for development of military products. (This would be a form of subsidy.) The implications of this kind of financing would have to be considered in any agreement to reduce military expenditures.

# Bibliography

Aleksandrov, A. M., *Gosudarstvennyi Biudzhet SSSR,* Moscow, 1961.

Allakhverdian, A. M., and Liubimov, N. N., eds., *Finansy SSSR,* Moscow, 1958.

Allakhverdian, D. A., *Finansy v Period Stroitel'stva Kommunizma,* Moscow, 1961.

_____, ed., *Finansy SSSR,* Moscow, 1962.

Allakhverdian, D. A., et al., *Problemy Finansovogo Planirovaniia,* Moscow, 1963.

Atlas, M., *Razvitie Gosudarstvennogo Banka SSSR,* Moscow, 1958.

Batyrev, V., Kaganov, G., and Iagodin, I., *Organizatsiia i Planirovanie Denezhnogo Obrashcheniia v SSSR,* Moscow, 1959.

Becker, Abraham S., *Soviet Military Outlays since 1955,* The RAND Corporation, RM-3886-PR, Santa Monica, Calif., July 1964.

_____, *Soviet National Income, 1958-1964.* University of California Press, Berkeley and Los Angeles, 1969, Chapter 7.

Bergson, Abram, *Soviet National Income and Product in 1937,* New York, Columbia University Press, 1953.

_____, *National Income and Product of Soviet Russia Since 1928,* Cambridge, Mass.: Harvard University Press, 1961.

Boguslavskii, M., Greben', Ia., and Proselkov, A., *Bankovskii Uchet i Operatsionnaia Tekhnika,* Moscow, 1960.

Bornstein, Morris, "Inspection of Economic Records as an Arms Control Technique," *Journal of Arms Control,* October 1953.

Borodin, S., Demichev, A., and Rozin, P., *Finansy i Kredit,* Moscow, 1963.

Campbell, Robert W., *Accounting in Soviet Planning and Management,* Cambridge, Mass.: Harvard University Press, 1963.

Chapman, Janet, *Real Wages in Soviet Russia Since 1928,* Cambridge, Mass.: Harvard University Press, 1963.

Cohn, Stanley, "The Gross National Product in the Soviet Union: Comparative Growth Rates," *U.S. Congress, Joint Economic*

*Committee, Dimensions of Soviet Economic Power* (Hearings, December 10-11, 1962), Washington, D.C., 1962.

Davies, R. W., *The Development of the Soviet Budgetary System,* Cambridge, Eng.: Cambridge University Press, 1958.

Dedkov, R., *Razvitie Biudzhetnogo Ucheta,* Moscow, 1962.

Dymshits, I. A., et al., *Finansy i Kredit SSSR,* Moscow, 1956.

Gallik, Daniel, Jesina, Cestmir, and Rapawy, Stephen, *The Soviet Financial System: Structure, Operation and Statistics,* Foreign Demographic Analysis Division, U.S. Department of Commerce, Series P-90, No. 23, Washington, D.C., 1968, pp. 75, 167-181.

Gerashchenko, V. S., ed., *Denezhnoe Obrashchenie i Kredit SSSR,* Moscow, 1970.

Godaire, J. G., "The Claim of the Soviet Military Establishment," *U.S. Congress, Joint Economic Committee, Dimensions of Soviet Economic Power* (Hearings, December 10-11, 1962), Washington, D.C., 1962.

Henkin, Louis, *Arms Control, Issues for the Public,* Englewood Cliffs, N. J.: Prentice-Hall, 1961.

Holzman, Franklyn D., *Soviet Taxation: The Fiscal and Monetary Problems of a Planned Economy,* Cambridge: Harvard University Press, 1955.

_____, "Soviet Inflationary Pressures, 1928-1957," *Quarterly Journal of Economics,* May 1960.

_____, ed., *Readings on the Soviet Economy,* Chicago: Rand McNally, 1962.

Judy, Richard, "Information, Control and Soviet Economic Management," in *Mathematics and Computers in Soviet Economic Planning* (John Hardt et al., eds.), New Haven, Conn.: Yale University Press, 1967, pp. 1-48.

Kaliteevakaia, A. V., et al., *O Biudzhetnykh Pravakh Soiuza SSSR, Soiuznykh Respublik, i Mestnykh Sovetov Deputatov Trudiashchikhsia,* Moscow, 1963.

Kisman, N., and Slavnyi, I., *Sovetskie Finansy v Piatoi Piatiletke,* Moscow, 1956.

Kondrashev, D. D., *Tsena i Stoimost' v Sotsialisticheskom Khoziaistve,* Moscow, 1963.

Kostinsky, Barry, *Description and Analysis of Soviet Foreign Trade*

*Statistics,* Foreign Demographic Analysis Division, U.S. Department of Commerce, Washington, D.C., 1974.

Kovylin, V., *Nalog s Oborota po Promyshlennym Tovaram,* Moscow, 1963.

Krueger, Constance, "A Note on the Size of Subsidies on Soviet Government Purchases of Agricultural Products," *ACES Bulletin,* Fall 1974, Vol. 16, No. 2.

Lavrov, V. V., et al., *Gosudarstvennyi Biudzhet,* Moscow, 1961.

_____, *Finansy i Kredit SSSR,* Moscow, 1964.

League of Nations, Conference for the Reduction and Limitation of Armaments, National Defense Expenditure Commission, *Report of the Technical Committee,* Vols. 1-3, Geneva, 1933-1935. Conf. D. 158.

_____, *Draft Convention,* Geneva, 1934, Conf. D./C.G.160 (1).

Liando, A., *Voprosy Finansovogo Balansa Narodnogo Khoziaistva,* Moscow, 1963.

Melman, Seymour, *Inspection for Disarmament,* New York: Columbia University Press, 1958.

Moliakov, D. S., *Finansirovanie Narodnogo Khoziaistva,* Moscow, 1962.

Morozova, I. A., *Balans Narodnogo Khoziaistva i Metody ego Postroeniia,* Moscow, 1961.

Nimitz, Nancy, *Soviet National Income and Product, 1956-1958,* The RAND Corporation, RM-3112-PR, Santa Monica, June 1962.

_____. *Soviet Expenditures on Scientific Research,* The RAND Corporation, RM-3384-PR, Santa Monica, Cal., January 1963.

_____. *The Structure of Soviet Outlays on R & D in 1960 and 1968,* The RAND Corporation, Santa Monica, Calif., June 1974 (R-1207-DDRE).

Nolting, Louvan E., *Sources of Financing the States of the Research, Development, and Innovation Cycle in the USSR,* Foreign Economic Reports No. 3, U.S. Department of Commerce, Bureau of Economic Analysis, Washington, D.C., September 1973.

Notkin, A. I., ed., *Sotsialisticheskoe Nakoplenie: Voprosy Teorii i Planirovania,* Moscow, 1973, p. 222.

Nove, A., "Soviet Budgets After Stalin," *The Review of Economics and Statistics,* Vol. 36, No. 4, November 1954, pp. 415-424.

Nove, A., and Zauberman, Alfred, "A Soviet Disclosure of Ruble National Income," *Soviet Studies,* Vol. 2., No. 2, October 1959.

Plotnikov, K. N., *Biudzhet Sotsialisticheskogo Gosudarstva,* Moscow, 1948.

————, *Ocherki Istorii Biudzheta Sovetskogo Gosudarstva,* Moscow, 1955.

————, *Gosudarstvennyi Biudzhet SSSR,* Moscow, 1959.

Popov, V. F., ed., *Gosudarstvennyi Bank SSSR: Kratkii Ocherk k Sorokaletiiu Oktiabria,* Moscow, 1957.

Powell, Raymond Park, *Soviet Monetary Policy,* Unpublished Ph.D. dissertation, University of California, 1952.

————. "Recent Developments in Soviet Monetary Policy," *Readings on the Soviet Economy* (Franklyn D. Holzman, ed.), Chicago: Rand-McNally, 1962.

————, "Monetary Statistics," in V. G. Treml and J. P. Hardt, eds., *Soviet Economic Statistics,* Durham, N.C.: Duke University Press, 1967.

*Pravda,* Annual budget speeches (usually in December).

Rovinskii, N. N., ed., *Finansovoe Pravo,* Moscow, 1946.

Semenov, V. N., "Finansirovanie Sel'skogo Khoziaistva," *Finansy SSSR,* No. 5, 1974, pp. 37-47.

Shvarts, G., *Beznalichnyi Oborot i Kredit v SSSR,* Moscow, 1963.

SIPRI (Stockholm International Peace Research Institute), *World Armaments and Disarmament,* Cambridge, Mass.: MIT Press, 1974.

Sitnin, V. K., *Kontrol' Rublem v Sotsialisticheskom Khoziaistve,* Moscow, 1956.

Smirnov, A., *Ekonomicheskoe Soderzhanie Naloga s Oborota,* Moscow, 1963.

Sobol', V. A., *Ocherki po Voprosam Balansa Narodnogo Khoziaistva,* Moscow, 1960.

Sosnovy, Timothy, "The Soviet Military Budget," *Foreign Affairs,* No. 3, 1964, pp. 487-494.

Turetskii, Sh. Ia., ed., *Rasshirennoe Sotsialisticheskoe Vosproizvodstvo i Balans Narodnogo Khoziaistva,* Moscow, 1964.

USSR, Ministerstvo Finansov, Biudzhetnoe Upravlenie, *Raskhody Na Sotsial'no-Kul'turnye Meropriiatiia po Gosudarstvennomu Biudzhetu SSSR*, Moscow, 1958.

_____, *Gosudarstvennyi Biudzhet SSSR i Biudzhety Soiuznykh Respublik,* Moscow, 1962. Also 1966 and 1970 revised editions.

_____, *Mestnye Biudzhety SSSR,* Moscow, 1960.

USSR, Tsentral'noe Statisticheskoe Upravlenie, *Narodnoe Khoziaistvo SSSR, Statisticheskii Ezhegodnik,* Moscow, published annually (called *Narkhoz*)

USSR, Tsentral'noe Statisticheskoe Upravlenie, *Narodnoe Khoziaistvo SSSR, 1922-1972,* Moscow 1972.

U.S., Central Intelligence Agency. *The 1960 Soviet Budget,* November, 1960.

_____. *The Soviet Budget for 1961,* June 1961.

_____. *The Soviet Budget for 1962,* November 1962.

U.S., Congress, Joint Economic Committee. *Dimensions of Soviet Economic Power, Hearings Together with Compilation of Studies, December 10-11, 1962,* Washington, D.C., 1962.

Volodarskii, L. M. *Statistika i Planirovanie Promyshlennosti,* Moscow, 1960.

Wallis, W. Allen, and Roberts, Harry V. *Statistics: A New Approach,* Glencoe, Ill.: Free Press, 1956.

Zverev, A. G. *Natsional'nyi Dokhod i Finansy SSSR,* Moscow, 1961.

## About the Author

**Franklyn D. Holzman** received the Ph.D. in economics from Harvard University in 1952. His dissertation dealt with the Soviet financial system and was published under the title *Soviet Taxation: The Fiscal and Monetary Problems of a Planned Economy* (Harvard University Press, 1955). He has also written on inflation theory and foreign trade theory and is a leading authority on the trade of communist nations, which is the subject of his recent book, *Foreign Trade Under Central Planning* (Harvard University Press, 1974). Professor Holzman began his teaching career at the University of Washington in Seattle. He is a professor in the Department of Economics and the Fletcher School of Law and Diplomacy, Tufts University, as well as a research associate of the Russian Research Center, Harvard University. He served as a consultant to the United States Arms Control and Disarmament Agency from 1964 to 1974.